Chief of the Chiefs

Louis Rooks Bruce
Mohawk/Sioux,
Commissioner of Indian Affairs
and Lobbyist

Jane Richardson

Cover illustration:
"Cheyenne Bear Hunter"
Bronze Sculpture and Photo
by James A. Ford
www.JamesAFord.com

Thistle Publishing, Shelby Twp., Michigan

Chief of the Chiefs
Louis Rooks Bruce
Mohawk/Sioux, Commissioner of Indian Affairs and Lobbyist

by
Jane Richardson

Published by

Thistle Publishing
11985 Cherokee Circle, Suite 218
Shelby Township, MI 48315
www.thistlepub.com

Printed in the United States of America.

Publisher's Cataloging-In-Publication Data
(Prepared by The Donohue Group, Inc.)

Richardson, Jane.
  Chief of the chiefs : Louis Rooks Bruce : Mohawk/Sioux, Commissioner of Indian Affairs and lobbyist / Jane Richardson ; cover illustration, "Cheyenne bear hunter," bronze sculpture and photo by James A. Ford.

  p. : ill., facs. ; cm.

  ISBN: 978-1-879403-18-5

1. Bruce, Louis Rooks. 2. United States. Bureau of Indian Affairs--Officials and employees--Biography. 3. Mohawk Indians--Biography. 4. Dakota Indians--Biography. 5. Indians of North America--Government relations. 6. Lobbyists--United States--Biography. I. Ford, James A. (James Allen), 1950- II. Title. III. Title: Louis Rooks Bruce

E93 .R53 2008
970./00497/092   2007909763

Dedication

To all American Indians ...

...past and present.

Contents

Chief of the Chiefs

Acknowledgements

With grateful thanks to all members of the Bruce family who so proudly shared their deepest feelings. And to their friends who joyously added memories, but are too numerous to mention individually for fear of inadvertently omitting someone.

However, there must be special thanks to Alexander (Sandy) MacNabb for endless hours, weeks and months of dedication, reliving the awesome past, of work with his dear friends and colleague, Louie, and unselfishly sharing his knowledge and documentation.

To Tom Oxendine, the "angel on the Commissioner's shoulder;" who knew the Commissioner's every move and thought, and tirelessly shared those precious memories.

To Bradley Patterson, who generously brought the White House actions into the book, sparking it with reality.

To Trail of Broken Treaties and AIM members for their clarifying viewpoints.

To Ernest Benedict, the Mohawk who brought their past into the present with his astute clairvoyance and charm.

To the many museum curators and educators for their enthusiastic support and tireless assistance.

To my son Bob for relentless endeavors to make this work of the finest quality, in our joint hope of better understanding our fellow man; and to daughter Barbara for the loan of her ear and shoulder.

To my husband George for his encouragement and devotion in helping me to capture the essence of two American Indians, each of whom had struggled to better the lives of all Native Americans.

Jane Richardson
Cooperstown, NY

Introduction

By Sandy MacNabb, former Asst. Commissioner of
Indian Affairs

Like the miner's canary, the Indian marks the shifts from
fresh air to poison gas in our political atmosphere; and our
treatment of Indians, even more than our treatment of other
minorities, reflects the rise and fall of our democratic faith.

Felix Cohen

The Political Atmosphere of the
Twentieth Century
The Franklin Roosevelt Years

When John Collier took office as Commissioner of
Indian Affairs in 1933, Congress was considering the
Wheeler-Howard Act, later passed into law in 1934.
Formally known as the Indian Reorganization Act, it
was in fact a "New Deal" for Indians. Authored
principally by Attorney Felix Cohen in the Interior
Department Solicitor's Office with help from the
Office of Indian Affairs.

The Act reversed the harmful Dawes Act of 1887
which facilitated Indian lands decreasing from
113,000,000 acres in 1887 to 47,000,000 shortly
thereafter. At the same time, tribal funds had decreased from $500,000,000 to $12,000,000. Ironi-

cally much of these funds were directed at paying the administrative costs of the Bureau of Indian Affairs.

The past century has witnessed two presidential administrations that had policies which were friendly towards American Indian rights. They were Franklin D. Roosevelt and that of Richard M. Nixon. Certainly not two peas in a pod, yet Presidents who shared a desire to make the nation friendlier for its first inhabitants. They not only felt this way but they put people in office to carry out these intentions. Louie Bruce was one of these people.

The longest serving officer in Franklin Roosevelt's cabinet was Harold L. Ickes who began his political life as a member of Theodore Roosevelt's Bull Moose Party in Chicago. He then became active in Republican politics and generally thought of as a moderate.

A strong supporter of minority rights, Ickes had been president of the Chicago NAACP. He introduced Marian Anderson at the Lincoln Memorial when the Daughters of the American Revolution denied her the use of Constitution Hall. He was an outspoken critic of the Japanese internment in the '40s and was considered to be the Roosevelt administration's preeminent liberal. He had the proper credentials to be a favorable link in the political chain that was needed to support changes that were long overdue in the relationships between the government of the United States and the Indian Tribes.

The appointment of John Collier as Commissioner of Indian Affairs in 1933 brought an outspoken critic of government Indian policy to the center of Indian and U.S. governmental relationships. Collier went on record as wanting to restore Indian tribal rights, customs and land.

The Stormy Political Atmosphere
of the Nixon Years

Then in the late 1960s and early 1970s things began to happen. It all may have started with *Our Brother's Keeper: the Indian in White America*. It is an early 70s indictment of the government of the United States dealing with American Indian Tribes and people. This thoughtful but alarming book was written by Edgar Cahn, a white law professor and several American Indian activists, including: Ernie Stevens (Oneida), Jerry Wilkerson (Cherokee), and Browning Pipe Stem (Otoe-Missouria) who later became part of the core of the BIA reform group.

Or, it could have been started with Bill King, the n/i (Bureau of Indian Affairs code for non-Indian) the BIA Agency Superintendent at the Salt River Pima-Maricopa Community in Arizona. He began to let contracts to the tribes to run their own programs and take charge of their own affairs.

But, then maybe it was Alvin Josephy, Editor of the American Heritage who wrote two very detailed articles for the New York Times detailing the problems in Indian Country. These articles not only penetrated the Nixon White House but they were frequently quoted by senior White House Staff.

In reality, it was all of this and much more that was sending clear signals to the people in power, President Nixon and his White House staff. The message was clear; change was overdue in the way our government dealt with Indian people. President Nixon was open to suggestions. Some say it was due to his early association with a Native American coach. Richard M. Nixon; President of the United States, wanted to make things better for Indians and went about staffing his White House and Interior Department with folks that do just that. Feeling the winds of change the President issued a license for change.

The White House staff had determined that the old BIA was almost beyond repair and they set about replacing the BIA senior staff with young Indian and non-Indian activists, several of whom were attorneys and other professionals. This done, they soon were being called "The New Team."

There had been a rather extensive Commissioner search. It took time and the White House staff grew impatient while many of the BIA Regional Directors (they were called Area Directors in those days), had served terms as Acting Commissioner. This became so prevalent that they referred to themselves as members of "Actors Equity." So there was always someone to run the train but it was always the same old train, nothing was changing, or at least not fast enough for the White House. They wanted a new Indian from the outside, hopefully a Republican, but what ever, they wanted one who would make changes, and reform the old War Department step child, the Bureau of Indian Affairs. Then they found Louie Bruce.

The White House liked Louie. He was a Republican, an Indian, a fresh and smiling face, popular with the Indians and one of the founders of the National Congress of American Indians (NCAI), the oldest and largest Indian organization in the nation. Louie had been a rather well known college athlete and had run youth programs during FDR's administration. So Louie was anointed Commissioner. There was some negative criticism about him being a Greenwich Indian, but that soon passed.

Louie Bruce served from 1969 through 1973 and he laid the groundwork with the Administration and Congress for the Indian Self Determination – Education Assistance Act, which rivals Commissioner Collier's Indian Reorganization Act for importance and value to Indian people. Also, in the Louis Bruce term came the acceptance of Indian preference policy, following the decision in Mancari v. Morton, which established the fact that preference to Indians in BIA personnel actions is not racial but based on the right to self-government.

After the White House center of power came the Secretary of the Interior. They searched for one who would be open to reform and settled on Walter Hickel, businessman and former Governor of Alaska, who was viewed as a supportive friend of Alaska Natives. The term Alaska Native included: Indians, Aleuts and Eskimos. Having refused Nixon's first request he agreed to take on the job of Secretary of the Interior the second asking and served from January of 1960 through Thanksgiving Eve, the 25th of November 1970, when he was called to the White House and fired for publicly opposing the Administration's Viet Nam policy.

Hickel revealed his strong backing of the Native population when other members of the Nixon cabinet criticized the Alaska Native Claims Settlement Act and when other cabinet officers objected to the draft bill stating that it was not economically and legally sound; Hickel agreed but added that it was morally sound. Hickel prevailed.

Rogers Morton was a wealthy, 6'5" tall, gentleman from Maryland who succeeded Wally Hickel. He was a former Republican Congressman and, like his brother, a former Chairman of the Republican National Committee. Secretary Morton's term at Interior lasted from January 29, 1971 until April 3, 1975.

After the BIA headquarters takeover by some members of the American Indian Movement (AIM), he became more concerned about reforming the government relationship with Indian tribes and people. He supported the Indian Road Construction program and the Indian Action Teams, which set up Indian construction companies.

The Congress of the United States, an Atmosphere unto Itself

Congress always seemed to want to have a controlling vote regarding Indians. But then what about the Indian people; how did they feel about changing things? Maybe losing any relationship with the federal government, even though it was sort of a love/hate relationship, like Elmer Gantry, it still was real and set Indians off from other so-called minorities? Then what about the general public; did they even understand the basic federal relationship with the Indian Nations and Tribes, or did they think it was all some welfare programs? What about the friend of Congress, business interests who wanted more and more of the Indian resources?

Article I of the Constitution of the United States deals with the Legislative Branch of our government. Section 8 of that Article sets out the Powers of Congress, and provides:

> The Congress shall have the Power to Lay and collect Taxes, Duties, Imposts and Excises, to pay the Debts and provide for the common Defence and general Welfare of the United States but all Duties, Imposts and Excises shall be uniform throughout the United States.
>
> To borrow money on the credit of the United States;
>
> **To regulate Commerce with foreign Nations, and among the several States, and with the Indian Tribes;**

This is the only mention of Indians or Indian Tribes in the U.S. Constitution. That's it. But out of this grew some very complicated laws and arrangements and two thick volumes of the United States Code. Nevertheless the way things were going the Indians always seem to lose — except in the movies.

Louis Bruce: The Commissioner
of Indian Affairs

This is the story of an American Indian named Louis Rooks Bruce whose father, Dr. Louis Bruce, was a dentist, an ordained Methodist minister, and a Chief of the Mohawk Indian Nation and whose mother was an Oglala Sioux. It is the portrait made from many mosaic segments of his life. Upon examination he seems to be a rather ordinary man. Yet he ran one of oldest and largest bureaucracies in Washington. How then does such a life bring a man to some truly extraordinary accomplishments as Commissioner of Indian Affairs?

What brought Louis Bruce, a gentle and mild mannered man, to this job? He had set pole-vaulting records in college and had previously modeled men's clothing for the Rogers Peet Company of New York. Called to Washington at a time of the American Indian protest and confrontation, many asked why was this Indian from Greenwich Village the answer to the militant Alcatraz takeover?

What then brought John Collier, President Roosevelt's Commissioner of Indian Affairs (1933-1945), to that same job, almost a half-century earlier? Collier was a New York social worker, with a burning desire to protect Indian lands and restore Indian culture and heritage, but with little practical bureaucratic experience.

How were they alike? They both had an overriding dream to make America a better place for Indian people. Or, if they were not alike what was similar in the larger political environment in which they journeyed?

What about these ordinary qualities? We all are somewhat accustomed to reading or hearing about very talented people who may have risen from rather obscure beginnings to levels of greatness. But these two people, Louie Bruce and John Collier, were not such people. They were rather ordinary people with ordinary experiences but two people who shared a dream, a dream for a better life for American Indians.

My life has been greatly enriched by a few truly great people that I have known. These included Eleanor Roosevelt, Kathryn Anne Porter, Arnold Toynbee, Dee Brown, and a monsignor of the Roman Catholic Church named Tom. These great people, up close seemed very ordinary. I have often thought that such ordinary qualities seem to be almost a require-ment for great accomplishments. No time to acquire a glitzy finish, no time to take bows, no finely spun press releases and cute demonstrations in the end zone. But all of these people did have two common qualities. One, they appeared to me to be very ordi-nary and two, they were both very goal oriented.

I would like to add one more name to this list or at lease suggest it for your consideration. Louie Bruce. You be the judge. Wait, please make your decision after you finish this book, and see then if you can define what makes a Commissioner of Indian Affairs a great commissioner.

The answer to this question, I am sure, has some-thing to do with the political atmosphere in which they operated, who they worked for and the mood of the White House regarding Indians. How did the Secretary of the Interior feel about reforming one of his subordinate agencies, especially the one that had been acquired from the War Department?

Then there were the other federal agencies, the ones that wanted to run roads through Indian land because it would cost less. Or the agencies that wanted to, and did, put up dams that backed up water on Indian land.

Running the Reformers and
The Indian Self Determination – Education
Assistance Act.

If the Indian Reorganization Act was the crowning jewel of John Collier's stewardship of the BIA, it saved Indian tribal governments, then the Indian Self Determination - Education Assistance Act is the crowning jewel of Louie Bruce's term as Commissioner of Indian Affairs. It put tribal governments in charge of their own destiny and did not destroy the trust relationship.

Even though not enacted by a friendly Congress, until after Louie's departure, it was still the core of Louie Bruce's efforts at the Bureau. He always kept this dream in focus. I never saw him complain about antagonists, whether governmental or private, Indian or white. The only time I ever saw him angry was when others wanted to give up. Then his anger was fury and it was immediate. He kept us all moving forward. His secret weapons were love and understanding, I am sure lessons that he grew up with, taught by his Methodist minister father. Always for Indians, never seeking credit or praise, Louie Bruce accomplished new legislative heights for Indian tribes and people. Louie never felt important; he knew that he was ordinary, but he also knew that his mission was not ordinary. He knew in his heart that if he did not succeed in realizing his dream of letting Indian people run their own affairs it would be years before anyone tried again.

Thank you, Louie.

Sandy MacNabb
Former Assistant Commissioner of
Indian Affairs,
and a practicing attorney of Canadian
Micmac (Mi'kmaq) Indian descent

Louis Rooks Bruce, about 1960

The Mohawk Tribe and St. Regis Reservation

C hief of the Chiefs." That's what the younger Louis Bruce used to say to his family. His far-reaching dream was to help make a difference to his Native American people. When he received President Nixon's invitation to become Commissioner of Indian Affairs, he triumphantly declared his mission was about to come true. Later President Richard Nixon mirrored the discerning views of thousands in his letter to Louis, expressing, "Thanks to your splendid efforts, we have set a new course in Indian affairs."

What brought this Mohawk/Sioux Indian to the imposing position of Commissioner of Indian Affairs? The cumbersome road for Louis and his forebears took many jagged twists; the journey could have been painful, long, full of foreboding, yet Louis filled it with unbounded enthusiasm, wonderful education, enlightenment and cultural changes. Through it all, his warm helping hand was always extended to both Native Americans and non-Indians. Perhaps one cannot fully appreciate this gregarious man without first knowing his father, mother, grandparents and their Mohawk and Sioux backgrounds.

The senior Louis Bruce was born January 16, 1877 on a small farm near the St. Regis Reservation in New York State near the Canadian border. His mother, Christina Benedict Bruce, aka Kahawenonkie, was a Canadian Indian who could not speak English. His father, John, was a Mohawk, at one time Chief of St. Regis Reservation and originally from St. Andrews, Canada.

As a young man the younger Louis Bruce once wrote to a friend:

> ...In the earlier days (John Bruce) wanted to join the Canadian Army so badly that he lied about his age. He was too old to join but was accepted and was sent to Egypt. Never could find out any dates or how long he was in Egypt. He had asthma so severely he couldn't have been able to keep up.

> Grandma Bruce had always lived on Cornwall Island. She apparently had never attended school and couldn't speak English. Dad could not converse with his mother. He always had to have an interpreter. Dad had forgotten how to talk and understand Indian language.

The Iroquois called the region of the St. Lawrence River "The Garden of the Great Spirit."

Here the Indians could reap the bounties of nature, picking and eating, for one thing, the early blooming Spring Beauties, a lovely wildflower.

Still visible on this five mile east to west stretch of Cornwall Island are weathered cedar fence posts, an occasional old outbuilding and barns, silent among the very few working farms. Nearby on the mainland, several industrial plants have drastically ruined the land and polluted the water. Several lawsuits have failed to compensate the Native Americans for their loss of fertile soil and their fish.

Older structures on the Island still reflect the architecture of the early 1800s, nicely kept for over a century, the current Indians very proud of the workmanship of their ancestors. There remain many Benedicts living on the Island of approximately 5000.

Methodist Church, Cornwall Island

They enjoy recalling Grandfather Mitchell Sawen-nakarati Benedict, also a farmer, who lived to be close to 100. Mitchell was determined that it would be good to have a Methodist Church at hand, as well as a school. In 1870 he set aside some of his land for that purpose. Oral family history recounts that this was accomplished, providing a lease for 100 years and his personal commitment. Behind the barn in an open pasture a 20 ft. x 30 ft. white wooden church was erected. Sadly, it burned in 2003, presumably by arson. Near to its foundation the forlorn empty parsonage, however, remains standing in reverent silence.

Methodist Church after the fire

Near to it facing west and a short walk behind Mitchell's house reclines a simple headstone of Mitchell Benedict in what has become a family cemetery. He was the pastor in the neat clapboard church, and tenant of the parsonage. Members enjoyed coming to this little Methodist church from several nearby islands. In 1872 the Indian Agent listed the congregation at between 25 and 30 members. It took many of the parishioners to help with the construction, but interestingly, they did not tithe; the reason being they literally did not have money!

Some monies were made available through the Indian Agent due to interest accrued on some land that was leased by the Akwesasne (the Mohawk tribe).

Parsonage, Cornwall Island

This very generous man, Mitchell, also allowed land he owned below the church to be used to build a schoolhouse. A Mohawk led classes in both Mohawk and English. Methodist hymns were taught to eager children.

Sawennakarati (Mitchell Benedict's) daughter Kahawenonkie and her husband John Bruce had a son, the afore-mentioned Louis Bruce. Louis attended Carlisle Boarding School where he met his wife, (discussed in detail later in this book). But it was here at this little Methodist Church in which Louis Bruce would later come to visit and be a guest preacher.

Of added interest is the fact that Charles Benedict and his wife Julia loved singing together and translated some of their favorite hymns into the Mohawk language. They are still being sung today.

Mitchell Benedict's headstone, family cemetery, Cornwall Island.

Trying to compare the days of old with the more recent eras, a father of five with children from five to seventeen years of age told of his thoughts on their Cornwall Island School back in his elementary days. Ernie's son Lloyd Benedict is a man with an excellent vocabulary and a conspicuous grasp on life. He spoke of his deep regret that the Mohawks didn't have someone he could find written up in the history books, someone he could regard as his personal hero.

"Everybody should have a hero," Lloyd said sternly. "The Vikings have theirs, and there's Cabot and Cook. All dominant societies have someone."

But then he went on to speak of his early years in school. World War II had ended and the school on Cornwall hired a Polish man who had been a Colonel in the Polish Army. After the war he had no home to go to. Others like him either fled to England or came to North America. "He found his way to Canada and the Island," Lloyd said, "and thought we would be sympathetic because of the things which had happened to us. He told us half the Polish army and their families were displaced because Germany and Russia had made deals that there should be no Poland. He became the Principal at the Cornwall elementary school, but also taught Social Studies, or at least his version of how he thought things had taken place. He needed psychological help." Lloyd remarked disdainfully.

This Polish principal made claims of early discoveries in North America by the Vikings and other Europeans. That always rankled the Indians who are proud of having lived here for thousands of years, and appreciate the museums with artifacts to prove it.

When asked if the students stood up to the Polish teacher's dialogue, the disgruntled reply was "Yeah, and got beat up for it."

"Would he beat the girls, too?"

"No, just the guys. That was like in grade six; and that would be the last time those kids would be in school. You could say they had a five-and-a-half-grade education.

"That Polish teacher said to us, 'I speak ten languages fluently.' " Lloyd laughed heartily, adding, "English wasn't one of them."

Passionately he continued, "It was really hard listening to him."

The St. Regis Reservation is, for the most part, in New York State, however Cornwall Island is within Ontario, Canada. The island extends 21 by 19 miles in the St. Lawrence River. Octogenarian Ernie Benedict, wise beyond his years when it comes to ancestral history, advised it was some time after the Revolutionary War that they surveyed. "It's really a kind of short section that was called the 45th parallel. I keep reading and hearing things."

Ernest Benedict

"Our community was here long, long before the U.S. and Canada; before the surveyors. They needed a community and the St. Lawrence was about the dividing line. In 1842 to 1849 they surveyed. They decided on the 45th parallel and that cut through Cornwall Island.

"One time a guy by the name of Archibald McNeff was drunk. It was October and it was cold. He was to pack a lot of liquid refreshment," Ernie spoke with a twinkle in his eye and laughter in his voice. "So they were surveying in a marsh. They put a stick in the ground and were snaking around and were going to tie the line up at the other end and they missed it by a half mile. Well, I guess the government was happy about that. It was against the Akwesasne Indians. Our land was smaller and so it stayed that way. There was never another surveyor party to go correct that error."

Crossing the border between Canada and the States, to their own little island, sometimes several times a day, can be a tedious hassle for the Native Americans since September 11, 2001. At rush hours lines create a long wait. There is the story of one upset Indian who, along with his ancestors, had lived for centuries on the island. This Native, well-known by all the residents and the border guards, was again asked by a customs officer to see his I.D. The long-time resident quietly replied, "Let me see yours."

Taken aback, the guard hesitated and then questioned what he meant by that.

"You're the trespasser here. You're on my land."

When asked if the boundary lines couldn't be checked with old records, the reply was that the Indian Council had nothing to go back to from earlier times. "The only Indian representative we have here is someone related to people who were keeping the land. I think that up to 1840 any records they had would be referred to up in Kingston near the Thousand Islands. Now you would deal with Ottawa. A lot of Indians are working with the government there, just like they are in Washington. Just like when Louis (Rooks) Bruce was Commissioner there," Ernie Benedict explained in his gentle way. Then with pride in his voice and a straightening of the shoulders, he said, "And Louis was my second cousin."

Louis's Mohawk tribe was also known as the Akwesasne. (Actually those living on the Canadian side are called the Mohawk Nation; those in New York State are called the Mohawk Tribe.) They were and are an integral part of the Iroquois Conference, the Conference consisting of six tribes or nations, each with a common culture and social structure and abiding by the same laws. They are the *Mohawk* (People of the Flint, Keeper of the Eastern Door), the *Oneida* (People of the Standing Stone), the *Onondaga* (People of the Hills, Keeper of the Central Fire), the *Cayuga* (People of the Great Pipe), the *Seneca* (People of the Great Hill, Keeper of the Western Door) and the *Tuscarora* (People of the Long Shirts).

Their lives and livelihoods were similar — a woodlands people, hunters and fishermen. They were known long years ago as the Longhouse people. A village could have consisted of as few as two longhouses and in earliest times were generally constructed near a stream. Later they were better protected from invading tribes if they were built atop hills.

Reproduction of palisade and longhouse is at Tsiionhiakwatha Archaeological site near St. Anicet, Quebec. (a.k.a. Drouler's site). This Akwesasne Mohawk site is dated approximately 1450 A.D. An interpretation center is open to the public. Pictures courtesy of their Museum.

Around the villages of the Mohawks were wooden palisades with watchtowers. These palisades, or outer walls, were constructed of their longest poles.

The longhouses within these "fortresses" were built to house anywhere up to 60 persons — ranging from perhaps 25 feet to 150 feet in length. Long poles would have been twisted solidly into the earth in two rows, ten or twelve ft. apart. They were then tied together at the top, while other poles were lashed together across them. These poles were tied together with bark, forming the outer wall of the house. A door at the end was hung with the skin of an animal.

Mike Tarbell, a Mohawk of the Turtle Clan and Museum Educator of the Iroquois Indian Museum in Howes Caves, New York advises that the Haudeno-saunee primarily stopped building longhouses around 1750 in the Mohawk Valley (Valley of the Crystals). However those living in the St. Lawrence Valley used longhouses far longer and lived in Hem-lock log houses. A fact, Mr. Tarbell stated, which is just recently coming to light, adding that "after the Revolution the Longhouse was used solely for social, political and religious gatherings."

The hemlock log house was surely a fantastic piece of work. Mike Tarbell states, "The chinking was completed with a mixture made from the cedar ashes, salt and water to form a concrete. This was spread between the logs. Once this had dried, the needles from the hemlock were brewed into a tea and then spread on the side of the house. This drew the resin from the logs and sealed up the house."

As a child, this author learned to respect the intel-ligence of our forebears, no matter how odd or "far out" a story, discussion or actions seemed. Mike's grandmother fit that bill, as well. That revered woman brewed the same hemlock tea for Mike when he had colds as that used to seal the houses.

The inside of these dwellings consisted of a long path down the middle, with an opening in the "roof" for smoke to escape from the fires beneath. Along the outer wall would be placed a seat for the family members, under which would be stored any clothing or necessities. This seat would also serve as a bed. Leather or skins were hung as an inner "wall" for privacy and separated family groups. These private family areas usually were approximately six feet by nine feet.

Besides being hunters and fishermen, they grew their fresh vegetables but found it necessary to move their longhouses every ten or twelve years, realizing the soil could no longer handle the same crops for extended periods.

Life Chief Ernie Benedict, seated in his neat wooden century home on Cornwall Island clearly remembers their ancient history and endless tales of early Indian life as told by their elders. Of the senior Louis Bruce's father, John, and his trip to Egypt, he stated, "Things were very informal then. There was a British expedition into Africa and the British were beaten up by the Sudanese. The general said 'Come and rescue me.' It was the British Army which confronted John, seeking his help. Apparently John was so skilled at riding the St. Lawrence rapids which once existed, his knowledge would be of tremendous help to the British on the Nile."

Unfortunately Chief Ernie Benedict did not know what happened to the British army or the rescue group. However he holds his cousin John in very high regard. These men had also shared the same grandfather.

Ernie's younger son was seated in silence across the room, listening intently to the dissertation. "So I think your grandfather and young Benedict were born here a couple hundred yards up the hill."

Cousins Lloyd and Don sat wistfully thinking back. Don Bruce asked, "How do you lay claim to a piece of property? Who is to say that somebody else didn't lay claim to the same piece of property?"

"There weren't that many Indians," Ernie responded with a broad smile. "But you had to lay claim because if you didn't the white man was going to come over and lay claim."

Don asked, "But who said that this was initially Indian territory?"

"The Mohawks who were living here."

"They selected this area to live?" Don asked.

"Yeah, a few thousand years ago!"

Chief Ernie is a wealth of Indian knowledge. He continued, "Remember when I was showing you those spear points? They were fashioning those spear points maybe 20,000, 25,000 years ago. Canada found some. They're up in the Museum in Ottawa. They were from up here in the Island. That was the ice age when they made them. And our elders told us where we came from. We didn't come from the north. We came from the south. You know, as the world is getting warmer the ice is receding and the earth is getting warmer."

Another Islander recounted his visit to and work in Belize with the Mayans. "Those Indians and we are not much different from each other. Even our languages sound similar," he said.

Ernest Benedict continued, "On those spear points? They know the stones were not from around here. They got traded for something. There was already some sort of a river system, [for people to travel] you know."

"Roots run deep," the Chief added most seriously.

"I wish I knew more about my roots," Don Bruce said in all sincerity.

"You can pick your friends, but you can't pick your relatives," Ernie's laughter echoed through their neat living room.

Don was particularly interested in how time was spent when Ernie was but a youngster — whether his father took him hunting or fishing.

"A little bit," he responded. "I think I was 10 or 11. Yeah, I was 11. My grandmother was getting elderly. She was living by herself and so I went over and tried to stay with her for 4, 5 years. Doing her work for her, I had to go into the woods, gathering up wood for the fire. And I did various things like picking berries, strawberries and corn and just a young handyman. And, uh, when my grandmother died we moved over to the village of Hogansburg and we did have a garden and I had to keep the weeds down. There weren't very many big activities; there weren't many jobs. Part of the time you would be a lumberjack, part of the time you worked on a farm 50, 60 miles away."

"In Canada?" Don asked.

"No. Growing up most of the work was on the American side."

It is certainly a well-known fact that the Akwesasne Mohawk are world renowned for their bravery and skill as ironworkers. The Akwesasne newspaper dated December 13, 2006 in an article titled: *Ratiristakehron: Mohawk Ironworkers* states in small part:

> Many people believe that the Mohawk men have a genetic immunity to heights. They believe that walking 30 stories above the city is something Mohawk men have no fear of. Men say, "It is more likely the rush of freedom they feel walking in the clouds."

Regarding the language most commonly used, Ernie explained that at the present time only about 10% speak Mohawk, their native tongue. But he quickly added, "When I was a kid almost everybody did. About 90%. And some of our kids were sent off to one of those residential schools."

"Were you?"

"No."

"Who determined who was sent to those schools?" Ernie was asked.

"Over where we were, on the American side, mostly it was one member of a family. Uh, if a mother or a father had died and only one parent left, a child would be picked."

We wondered if that was something our government decided, and Ernie replied, without changing his tempo and tone, "Yeah, almost every time it took pressure down."

Don persisted in the questioning. "Was it because the parent couldn't take care of all the kids? Or was it that they wanted the kids to be brought up better educated?"

He responded, "Very often it was the kid from a parent who wasn't able to take good care of them, and often it was because the father was a drunk. It was about 1900 when the residential schools were started. Things were bad. That was about the time, too, when there were a lot of epidemics. You never knew which one would go."

Nowadays the charm of the longhouse is a thing of the past. While a few can still be found in and around New York State, the more "modern" facilities are wooden houses, as introduced with the formation of Indian Reservations on which many Indians were forced to live.

Ernie Benedict introduced us to the Cornwall Island longhouse, used for social and religious events. Other houses on the island are the same now as any other small town or village in the States. Their home is neat as a pin, showcasing various Indian arts, handicrafts and memorabilia. Of special interest were some baskets. Asked the principal material used in that region, it was learned that although aromatic grasses were dried and turned into lovely baskets, of prime use by those we met were the wooden strips from the black ash tree.

Checking out the laborious procedure, a greater appreciation of the finished product evolves. After a tree is felled, strips are cut and pounded. A fine strip, perhaps a yard long by perhaps an inch wide, is then again split into two strips, half the initial gauge or thickness. It appeared this pliable pale cream-colored sliver of a tree was smooth, but no. Not to a professional basket weaver. It was next held on the aging knee of the craftswoman to be scraped and scraped until it was as soft as velvet, all minute, unseen "bumps" or "blemishes" removed.

The piece was then ready to be split down its length to whatever width the artisan needed for the basket or its decoration. Various shapes, sizes and decorative aspects come into play. Baskets can be useful or decorative. Whatever the aim of the weaver, they always seem to turn out beautifully. A favorite was the unusual shape and weave of one particular item appearing as an oversized thistle — bumps and all. It was truly a work of art, created by Ernie's wife, Florence.

On another visit Ernie spoke slowly and distinctly: "I was born on a farm and the family was moving to the American side when I was young. There was a farm there then and there's a gas station there now. My father was never able to get enough money to build a house. But my grandfather owned this farm. He got very old and so my father came here. We never owned any land."

Asking for more details about the farm, Ernie folded his hands under his chin and thoughtfully replied that it was just a general kind of farm, cattle and they raised mostly corn and oats.

Wondering how the tribes sustained themselves before the aluminum plant was built nearby on the mainland many years ago, Ernie advised it was mostly through agriculture. The entire region knew only a meager existence. And the nearby U.S. factories employed only a small number of Indians.

There was once a lacrosse factory built on the island, lacrosse being the old standby in Indian sports for centuries. Although the origins of the game are unknown, it is known, however, that it was a game of thanksgiving to the Creator for all their blessings. Scores of people could play at a time and some games covered many miles. Today its religious connotations are lost.

Sticks were made of wood, generally ash. Now they are made of titanium or kryptolyte, and their large Cornwall Island company is no more. However there is still a small company on the island which holds to the old standards except for replacing the wooden heads with something less dangerous to the player. Lacrosse is still a fast moving sport!

Most Indian clothing had been made of deerskin, the women wearing skirts, vests and moccasins. Both men and women's moccasins were made of leather for cold weather and sometimes made of cornhusks. Up north they wore leggings and breechcloths. In the winter they wore capes or shawls made of rabbit fur. In the winter the men wore leggings of leather and tunics. In the summer they shed the heavier clothing for cooler breechcloths.

Native American dances are different across the land. Here in the East the Mohawks claim their dancing is faster than that of the Plains Indians who move to the measured cadence of their drum. The people of St. Regis said their dance is "more processional, meaning they follow behind each other. It's faster, and at times they dance with partners. Frequently they are social and other times they are ceremonial — and definitely aerobic."

Even today these People of the Longhouse are governed by *The Great Law* which was devised perhaps as many as one thousand years ago. Its very essence is gentle and flows like a soft breeze. It unified these nations which did not speak the same language. It formed an alliance for Peace. It is felt that the United States Constitution and Canada should be indebted to the Iroquois nations for their freedom, although it is not recognized in such a way. In a manner of speaking, the U.S. House of Representatives and Senate resemble the setup of the Chiefs and others in the Indian Council.

Legend tells us there was a Tree of Peace which had long ago been planted on Onondaga property and in a 1977 translation of The Great Law of Peace it colorfully and poetically states:

> Under the shade of this Tree of Great Peace we spread the soft, white, feathery down of the Globe Thistle, as seats for you, Atotarho and your cousin statesmen.

> We place you upon those seats, spread soft with the feathery down of the Globe Thistle there beneath the shade of the spreading branches of the Tree of Great Peace. There shall you sit and watch the Fire of the League of Five Nations. All the affairs of the League shall be transacted at this place before you, Atotarho and your cousin statesmen, by the Statesmen of the League of Five Nations.

It should be noted that while there were originally five nations making up the Iroquois Confederacy, in the mid-1700s the Tuscarora moved north from the Carolinas and joined the group, making the current Six Nations.

They have their precise "Robert's Rules of Order" for their meetings, and are expected to conform accordingly. A small example:

> You Atotarho and your thirteen cousin Statesmen shall faithfully keep the space above the Council Fire clean, and you shall allow neither dust nor dirt to accumulate. I lay a long seagull wing before you as a broom.

The Council of the Mohawks, interestingly, is divided into three parts: the first to only listen to the discussion of the two other parties. The first party can call attention to any mistakes or errors. They then confirm the decisions and refer them to the Seneca statesmen for their decision. When the Seneca statesmen decide in accordance with the Mohawk statesmen, the problem then goes to the Cayuga and Oneida statesmen on the opposite side of the house.

Their Great Law of Peace further reads that when holding a Council, "the Onondaga statesmen shall open it by expressing their gratitude to their cousin statesmen, and greeting them, and they shall make an address and offer thanks to the earth, where men dwell; to the streams of water; the pools and the lakes; to the maize and the fruits to the medicinal herbs and to the forest trees for their usefulness; and to the animals that serve as food and give their pelts for clothing; to the great winds and the lesser winds; to the Thunderers; to the Sun, the mighty warrior; to the moon; to the messengers of the Creator who reveals his wishes; and to the Great Creator who dwells in the heavens above who gives all the things useful to men, and who is the source and the ruler of health and life." After these words of thanks, the Onondaga statesmen declare the council open.

Similar words of thanks are offered before smaller local councils. The following text is reprinted in part:

Greetings to the Natural World:
The Words Before All Else.

These words of thanksgiving come to us from the Native people known as the Haudenosaunee) also known as Iroquois or Six Nations, of upstate New York and Canada. The Thanksgiving Address has ancient roots, dating back over 1,000 years to the Foundation of the Great Law of Peace. ... A speaker is chosen to give the Thanksgiving Address. You are invited — encouraged — to share in these words, that our concentrated attention might help to rediscover our balance, respect, and oneness with nature.

Greetings to the Natural World

The People

Today we have gathered and we see that the cycle of life continues. We have been given the duty to live in balance and harmony with each other and all living things. So now we bring our minds together as one as we give greetings and thanks to each other as people.

NOW OUR MINDS ARE ONE.

The Earth Mother

We are all thankful to our Mother, the Earth, for she gives us all that we need for life. She supports our feet as we walk about upon her. It gives us joy that she continues to care for us as she has from the beginnings of time. To our Mother, we send greetings and thanks.

NOW OUR MINDS ARE ONE.

The Waters

We give thanks to all the Waters of the world for quenching our thirst and providing us with strength. Water is life. We know its power in many forms — waterfalls and rain, mist and streams, rivers and oceans. With one mind, we send greetings and thanks to the spirit of Water.

NOIW OUR MINDS ARE ONE.

The Fish

We turn our minds to all the fish life in the water. They were instructed to cleanse and purify the water. They also give themselves to us as food. We are grateful that we can still find pure water. So, we turn now to the Fish and send our greetings and thanks.

NOW OUR MINDS ARE ONE

The Plants

Now we turn to the vast fields of Plant life. As far as the eye can see, the Plants grow, working many wonders. They sustain many life forms. With our minds gathered together, we give thanks and look forward to seeing Plant life for many generations to come.

NOW OUR MINDS ARE ONE.

The Food Plants

With one mind we turn to honour and thank all the Food Plants we harvest from the garden. Since the beginning of time, the grains, vegetables, beans and berries have helped the people survive. Many other living things draw strength from them, too. We gather all the Plant foods together as one and send them a greeting and thanks.

NOW OUR MINDS ARE ONE.

The Medicine Herbs

Now we turn to all the Medicine Herbs of the world. From the beginning, they were instructed to take away sickness. They are always waiting and ready to heal us. We are happy there are still among us those special few who remember how to use these plants for healing. With one mind, we send greetings and thanks to the Medicine and to the keepers of the Medicine.

NOW OUR MINDS ARE ONE.

The Animals

We gather our minds together to send greetings and thanks to all the Animal life in the world. They have many things to teach us as people. We see them near our homes and in the deep forests. We are glad they are still here and we hope that it will always be so.

NOW OUR MINDS ARE ONE.

The Trees

We now turn our thoughts to the trees. The Earth has many families of Trees who have their own instructions and uses. Some provide us with shelter and shade, others with fruits, beauty and other useful things. Many people of the world use a Tree as a symbol of peace and strength. With one mind we greet and thank the Tree life.

NOW OUR MINDS ARE ONE,

The Birds

We put our minds together as one and thank all the Birds who move and fly about over our heads. The Creator gave them beautiful songs. Each day they remind us to enjoy and appreciate life. The Eagle was chosen to be their leaders. To all the Birds — from the smallest to the largest — we send our joyful greetings and thanks.

NOW OUR MINDS ARE ONE.

The Four Winds

We are all thankful to the powers we know as the Four Winds. We hear their voices in the moving air as they refresh us and purify the air we breathe. They help to bring the change of seasons. From the four directions they come, bringing us messages and giving us strength. With one mind, we send our greetings and thanks to the Four Winds.

NOW OUR MINDS ARE ONE.

The Thunderers

Now we turn to the west, where our Grandfathers, the Thunder Beings, live. With lightening and thundering voices, they bring with them the water that renews life. We bring our minds together as one to send greetings and thanks to our Grandfather, the Thunderer.

NOW OUR MINDS ARE ONE.

The Sun

We now send greetings and thanks to our eldest Brother, the Sun. Each day without fail he travels the sky from East to West, bringing the light of a new day. He is the source of all the fires of life. With one mind, we send greetings...

NOW OUR MINDS ARE ONE.

Grandmother Moon

We put our minds together and give thanks to our oldest Grandmother, the Moon, who lights the nighttime sky. She is the leader of women all over the world, and she governs the movement of the ocean tides. By her changing face we measure time, and it is the moon who watches over the arrival of children here on Earth...

NOW OUR MINDS ARE ONE.

The Stars

We give thanks to the stars who are spread across the sky like jewelry. We see them in the night helping the moon to light the darkness and growing things. When we travel at night they guide us home. ...

NOW OUR MINDS ARE ONE.

The Enlightened Teachers

We gather our minds together to greet and thank the enlightened Teachers who have come to help throughout the ages. When we forget how to live in harmony, they remind us of the way we were instructed to live as people...

NOW OUR MINDS ARE ONE.

The Creator

Now we turn our thought to the Creator, or Great Spirit, and send greetings and thanks for all the gifts of Creation. Everything we need to live a good life is here on this Mother Earth. For all the love that is still around us, we gather our minds together as one...

NOW OUR MINDS ARE ONE.

Closing Words

We have now arrived at the place where we end our words. Of all the things we have named, it was not our intention to leave anything out. If something was forgotten, we leave it to each individual to send such greetings and thanks in their own ways.

AND NOW OUR MINDS ARE ONE.

It is heart-warming to realize that during periods of great strife and endless hardships, time is taken to appreciate all the good things of life and the universe. Little wonder they gave thanks for animals and skins. Deerskin was not only made into clothing, but the bones were used to make rattles, needles for sewing and weaving. They made knives and hide-scrapers, awls, flutes and gaming dice from the bones, as well as hair combs. Indian mounds dating back 3000 years had bone hair combs, but this craft or art faded out in the 1800s when steel came into use for tools.

The animals provided plentiful food, and anything unusable was composted into the earth. A recycling, so to speak. Bear and elk were also abundant. Small creatures such as goose, duck, wild turkey, pheasant and other delicacies pleased their pallets when they could be found. For sweets, it was always a boon to come upon honey. A beautiful attribute of the Mohawk and others in the Iroquois Nation is their willingness to share their food. They have a great sense of cooperation.

Fish were abundant in this part of the world, with the St. Lawrence River, St. Regis and other rivers, numerous lakes and ponds. Sturgeon was a favored catch, for not only did the people enjoy its "meat," but also the caviar was a particular delicacy. The sturgeon was often smoked. Other fish in abundance were bass and perch. The exception to good fishing was the putrid waters surrounding Cornwall Island after installation of the three large American industries, as described earlier. To slightly compensate this condition and their local loss of fish, there are now a few "fish farms" for breeding.

Lloyd Benedict reported that at Easter season there is still some ice on the river, but if you take a boat out about 20 miles you can find good yellow perch.

In trying to picture the construction of a birch bark canoe as used by the Micmacs and other tribals, it was said they'd try to find a birch tree big enough so that the large piece of bark stripped from it would encircle the whole canoe. The smaller ends of bark could encompass the end of the watercraft. Pieces which needed to be sewn together would be done with materials from the roots of a spruce tree. They'd then "plaster" over the canoe with pine or spruce pitch.

In checking out local foods and recipes which had been handed down through time, it appears the use of corn in their special soups and breads is prominent. Also, one elder woman recounted her grandmother always fried her oatmeal before it was cooked. Any leftover oatmeal was made into patties the following day and refried. Of course absolutely nothing ever went to waste.

On the sparse island of Cornwall, one makes friends rapidly with a people gentle in manner, simple in lifestyle, their wealth abiding in a treasured heritage. Forebears are revered. Cousins are respected. Friends are welcomed. With deep regard they speak of their old guest preacher, Louis Bruce and of one even closer to them, his son Louis Rooks Bruce and his rise to fame in Washington, helping Native Americans across the nation on his journey through life.

Educating the
Native Americans
and
Louis' Baseball Career

L ouis Bruce (Sr.) in his later years penned *A Brief Sketch of Life*. He wrote: "It was my good fortune to spend at least 20 of my early years in Philadelphia. It came about in this way. My parents were Indian people (Mohawk) who lived in northern New York. An opportunity came to them to send two of their children to a school under the U.S. Government auspices. This school was located at 40th St. and Greenway Ave. near the Belmont Central City and 49th St. Station. About 100 boys, ages 7 to 20 attended the school."

This school was partly supported by the Episcopal Church. He attended it for two years, from its opening until it was closed by the government. He then attended two public schools before entering Central High School. It was while at the Boarding School that he met Nellie (Noresta) Rooks who was later to become his wife. She was from the Pine Ridge Reservation in South Dakota, one of several children who had come from the west to stay at the Educational House.

As an example of the austerity in government schools, the Pierre, S.D. institution issued two sets of clothes per child; one to wear while the other was being washed. It was said that if they could have had three sets, they would have been able to iron the clothes, but as it was they had to wear them with all the wrinkles.

With regard to their dwelling, there were neither curtains nor rugs on the floors and very few toys with which to play. Regarding bathing, it was done by grades and a child bathed only once every eighth day. The children were five to fifteen years old and classes were first through the eighth grade.

Unfortunately, in trying to "civilize" the Indian, as the government termed it, they felt they had to destroy all the Indian features, that is, their language, their clothing, their customs and anything to do with their culture. Boarding school was a part of "civilizing" them.

The following article, while being written for a specific area of schools, nonetheless reflects the sentiments applied well before and after the date indicated here. The May 20, 1897 edition of *The Evening Herald*, Syracuse, NY reads:

IMPORTANT TO THE INDIANS
Children of New York Reservations May Be Sent to Carlisle and Hampton

A matter of interest to the Onondaga Indians, as well as to the Indians on the other reservations of the State, is that Secretary of the Interior Bliss has just stated that hereafter, so long as he is in charge of the department, children of New York Indians who have arrived at such an age and degree of training as will fit them to appreciate the advantages of better educational facilities, shall be allowed the same privileges of other Indians with reference to the various non-reservation schools, including Hampton Institute and Lincoln Institute.

The Secretary of the Interior, without further legislation, has authority to pay the transportation and tuition of as many

Indian children as he deems proper to send to Carlisle and Hampton.

It is said that there are 2,400 children living on New York reservations of a school age, while more than 40 percent of them grow up in ignorance; that none of these children remained in school after attaining the age of fourteen years, and that these only obtained a smattering of the elementary studies; that the State furnished twenty-nine schools for the education of these Indians, but that they were of an inferior grade, the school buildings being without furniture or proper appointments and wholly unattractive to the Indian youth.

It would appear, however, that things were not necessarily equal at government schools across the nation. Eugene Rooks of South Dakota reports, "I went to two government schools. Life was good there. They were well regimented. We had to learn to march which prepared us for life in the Army. In the Government schools," he added, "they concentrated on academics and building character." He then went on to a Jesuit high school and to college in California before serving in World War II.

Referring back to Louis Bruce's abbreviated memoirs, he wrote, "In time a few of us were sent to the Central High School. Then, besides the regular studies, I played on its baseball and football teams. Our teams in those days ranked with the best in scholastic circles.

"We had a large playground and all kinds of competitive sports with baseball and football as the main items. Religious training and teaching were of minor importance. It was at this school that I became proficient at baseball. It was to be the means of advanced education. This school also made it possible for me to know Christian principles and Christian living.

"Our baseball opponents were Pennsylvania Charter, Germantown Academy, Central Manual Training,

Drexel Institute, and others. My baseball ability soon brought me larger engagements with semi-pro teams."

Louis Bruce, turn of the century.

Louis had graduated from Central High School, with third honors in his class. He was class Vice President in his senior year, captain of their baseball team and manager of their football team. Little wonder he was sports editor of their *Mirror*. Someone jokingly wrote of him, "Another good man gone wrong."

He started playing baseball in 1895 at Moiré's Station on the town team, and for eleven years with semi and professional teams, thereby paying his way through college. After Louis progressed through semi to his professional career he pitched for Atlantic City for two years. In 1900 he played with the Toronto, Canada National League team under the famous Manager Ed Barrow, before going to the Philadelphia Athletics of the American League, playing under Connie Mack.

Louis Bruce graduates from University of Pennsylvania, 1902.

Louis Bruce, pitcher, 1902.
Toronto Maple Leafs win the pennant.

Pitcher Bruce at extreme right of pitcher's mound, 1902

Teammates left to right: Gardner, Bruce, Briggs.

1902 Toronto Baseball Club – Louis Bruce, bottom right.

Indianapolis Sentinels
Back row, from left: McGready, Gromley, Ed Barrow,
Reidy, Weaver
Middle Row: Farrell, Martin, Thoney, Massey
Front row: Zalusky, Coach Carr, Morgan, Louis Bruce, Moran

In 1905 he moved to the American Association, again under Ed Barrow. His baseball career took him through 1907, spending the last two years with the Columbus American Association, followed by Rutland, Vermont's Northern League.

A weathered Associated Press article from a New York newspaper, written by Paul Mickelson, dated May 10th reads in small part:

Ed Barrow Reaches Three Score and Ten
and Looks Back Over Lively Career

Edward Grant Barrow, a gruff old timer who rose from the ranks of the peanuts to the ranks of the maker of world championship ball clubs for the New York Yankees was still going strong today as he reached his 70th birthday.

Over his 44 years as active manager, club president and big front office man, Barrow's teams have won ten American League pennants and seven World Championships — all of them with the Yankees, excepting the world title he captured with the Boston Red Sox in 1918.

Barrow considered Babe Ruth and Wagner to be great ballplayers but thought of Louis Bruce as the greatest "natural" player. He claimed Bruce could do everything well, feeling he could have become the greatest baseball star of them all.

A smattering of comments by the media over the years reads as follows:

Oct. 9, 1897 from *Sporting Life*: "Bruce, a full-blooded Indian pitched for Brandywine against Lancaster for four innings recently and not a semblance of a hit was made off his delivery. Piggy Ward says he is a wonder."

May 29, 1901 from *The Post Standard*, Syracuse. "Louis Bruce proved a puzzle to Montreal in his first game. Bruce pitched his best game for Toronto this season and had Montreal guessing all the time. Attendance: 700. Score: Toronto 4, Montreal 2."

June 27, 1902; *The Sporting News*: "Toronto Is On Top; Briggs and Bruce, the Premier Pitchers of Barrow's Team. ...Bruce is used in the outfield, owing to his prowess at the bat. He has hit safely in every game but one and his fielding is of the sensational order. Local scribes consider him the most valuable player in the Eastern Circuit."

Sept. 21, 1903; *Manitoba Free Press*, Winnipeg. "The Toronto baseball team management has sold the famous Canadian Pitcher, Louis Bruce, to Philadelphia National Club for $3,000."

Dec.31, 1903; *The Daily Review*, Decatur, Ill. "Everybody touts Bruce, the Indian secured by Connie Mack, as a marvel."

1904 *Spalding's Official Baseball Guide* (covering the 1903 season): "While Bruce and Massey were the hitters for Toronto, Bruce being a phenomenal man for the little Indian was played in some position almost every day on account of his ability to meet the ball."

Aug. 7, 1904, *The Washington Post.* "Indian Bruce has not come up to expectations, and Connie Mack probably will farm him out next season."

Sept. 18, 1904, *The Washington Post.* "Ollie Pickering of the Athletics will decorate the bench on the trip West. Bruce will take his place in center. Bruce bats better than Pickering."

April 4, 1905, *The Washington Post* "Connie Mack has sold Indian Bruce to the Indianapolis club."

This mighty ball player was but 150 pounds, standing 5 feet 5 inches, batting and throwing right handed.

Everyone, unfortunately, did not have Louis's skills and advantages to thrust him ahead in life. There is further interesting insight into the frightening transition for young Indian boys and girls, spanning their relatively safe life on a reservation to the unfamiliar dorms of government and public schools among strangers. Here, however, they were introduced to America's national, and favorite sporting pastime: baseball. This is clearly indicated in the following *Sporting News*, St. Louis, Mo., dated December 24, 1942. Chief Bender was interviewed by J. G. Taylor Spink, Editor. The article reads in small part:

Sent to Indian School in Philadelphia

"It was here in Philadelphia that I first learned to play ball at the age of 7," related the Chief. "That surprises you, doesn't it? My father and mother moved to the White Earth Reservation near Brainerd when I was about 4 and we settled on land that the government gave us. But it didn't work out very well under the Bender system of tilling the soil and we had a hard time of it.

"In Philadelphia at the time was a wealthy woman, a Mrs. Cox, who supported and conducted a school for Indian boys, from 7 to 15 years of age. It was called Lincoln Institute and was at Forty-ninth and Greeley Avenue, next to the Belmont Cricket Club.

"Mrs. Cox paid a visit to the White Earth Reservation and arranged to take me to Philadelphia. There were so many of us at home and so little to feed us that mother didn't mind giving me up."

Bender thought Lincoln Institute was just great, at first, having a good time there. He worked in the laundry as a way to help pay for his education and board. But more important to him, it was a chance to learn to play ball, to be with other kids his age, and he even learned how to make the balls, from core to cover.

Bender liked recalling the time when he was eight years old and thought he wanted to be a catcher. That idea faded quickly when he was hit between the eyes with a ball. In those days they had no means of protection. In fact, they didn't even have mitts at the school. For a catcher's glove he used a "dress-up" glove with the fingers cut off.

Bender continued to enjoy the game, more by watching the older boys play. "Louis Bruce was my hero!" he liked to boast.

He stayed at Lincoln Institute for five years, looking forward to the summer vacation months when he could go fishing or roam through open fields. But he quickly admits his favorite hobby was going out with a couple other boys and shooting bullfrogs down at the river.

After those five years Bender felt he had had enough of this life and wanted very badly to return to the reservation, his family and old friends. Mrs. Cox was kind enough to give him the money for the return trip and even packed a lunch for him. Before leaving the city he spent three of his dollars at the local hardware store, buying a shotgun.

There was another boy who felt much the same. His name was Seymour Fairbanks. The two of them took off together, lunches in hand. What a trip that must have been. They spent three days and nights on a train. Whenever it would stop they'd get off and do some shooting.

They enjoyed themselves as much as possible until reaching a place called Detroit, Minnesota (not Michigan). Bender had by this point spent all of his money; there was nothing left for the stagecoach fare to the White Earth Reservation. Luckily his young friend Fairbanks paid his fare. However, when he finally reached the reservation he had to walk the remaining 29 miles home, the trusty gun slung over his youthful shoulder.

It's impossible to know how many Indian boys and girls yearned to return to their old way of life and leave their schooling behind — and just how many Louis and Noresta Bruces there were, who took to furthering their education.

Louis Bruce marries
Noresta (Nellie) Rooks

L ouis Bruce, had saved enough money playing baseball to return to Philadelphia and enter the University of Pennsylvania, Department of Dentistry. After earning his D.D. degree in 1904, which he managed to do in three rather than four years, he practiced dentistry for two years in Syracuse, N.Y.

In his memoirs he wrote, "My heart's desire was not satisfied, so I decided to move along and get into the ministry." He felt this a far stronger "calling." Louis added, "I entered the Methodist Ministry and took special courses at Syracuse University. For 38 years I served 11 different churches in Central New York and Northern New York Conference of the Methodist Church."

On February 4, 1904, after having met Nellie, or Noresta, Rooks in school, they married in a ceremony held at St. Luke's Episcopal Church in Philadelphia. Of fascinating interest is the background of her parents.

Nellie's father was Joseph O. Rooks, a white man born in a log cabin in Unionville, Missouri on March 16, 1846. Joseph's mother was Temperance Mary Jackson who was 38 years of age at his birth. Joseph's father, John Rooks, was also 38 when Joseph was born.

Joseph was one of nine children and ran away from home to enlist in the Cavalry on August 10, 1861, fighting with the north. He served as a private in the Civil War in the Union Cavalry, Co. M, 7th Missouri, until Feb. 28, 1864.

Joseph then traveled west with other pioneers, stopping a little south of Cheyenne, Wyoming. He freighted for a living and in 1866 married Tigliska in Boxelder Creek, Colorado. Tigliska's father was a French trapper and her mother was a Sioux. In the custom of the day and region, the groom traded a horse for the bride. Their wedding was held in accordance with her tribal custom.

Joseph O. Rooks and wife, Kate

The year 1868 was a momentous one for Joseph who had become proficient in Indian languages. He was the interpreter for Chief Red Cloud when they both attended the 1868 Convention. He signed the Peace Treaty for Chief Red Cloud at Fort Laramie, Wyoming. Red Cloud had been the chief spokesman for all the tribes in that part of the United States, including Colorado, Wyoming, Nebraska and the

Dakotas. Red Cloud was a Sioux and they were the prominent tribe. [Red Cloud was the prominent Indian at the Wounded Knee conflict, of which you will read in the next chapter.]

Sadly, Joseph's lovely wife died during childbirth in 1872, delivering her third baby.

Grandmother Livermont (left) and Grandmother Kate Rooks, Dec. 1889.

On February 22, 1873 Joseph again married, the ceremony taking place at the Rosebud Indian Agency, performed by their Agent. This second wife was also a Sioux, named Kathryn (Kate) Robinson, a member of the Pine Ridge branch of the Sioux tribe. She was born November 16, 1855 in a covered wagon between Fort Laramie and Fort Robinson.

Kathryn and Joseph were married by the Rev. Hinman near the Spotted Tail Agency. Along with his first three children, they raised another 15, one of whom was Noresta (Nellie), born in 1878. The family moved to the Pine Ridge Reservation, a site of devastating historic significance, Wounded Knee.

Here Joseph worked for the Government as "Boss Farmer" from 1892 to 1900, where it was his job to hopefully take the bow and arrow away from the Indians and make farmers of them. He was later named Boss Farmer at Allen and in 1898 established a ranch in the Badlands, a rough country. Although there were ordinarily no white men allowed on this reservation, they were permitted to stay because of his wife.

Kate (dark dress) and Joseph (center front row)
with their 15 children

According to many old accounts, those were the days of endless rolling acres and sprawling miles of fenceless property. Herds of cattle and packs of horses could roam freely. Sadly, the white man indiscriminately killed off buffalo for their hides and tongues, leaving their remains to rot in the sun, a sacrilege by Indian moral standards. There were, thankfully, thousands of antelope on the flats and plenty of deer in the hills. Wolves, however, would sneak around in the night, killing the horses, or biting through their hamstrings. When that would happen the horses had to be shot. And it was certainly not unheard of to be clawed by a bear.

Then came the time when the government was issuing cattle to Indians. The Rooks received 18 cows, a bull and a team of mares. In those days there were tremendous grasslands for grazing, more than ample water available, and the Longhorn did exceptionally well. It had been the Army's job to parcel out the land, after doing all the surveying.

The original Rooks homestead, 1881. Louis Bruce's mother's birthplace, 18 miles from Kadoka, South Dakota

It is said that Joseph sold his ranch about the time of the First World War, including 650 head of cattle and 350 horses — all of which came from that original start back in 1890. He died in 1919 at the age of 73, and is interred at Fairview Cemetery, Kadoka, SD.

His wife Kate lived another seven years, dying in 1926 in Yankton, South Dakota at the age of 70, the mother of 15 children. Kate never had any schooling, nor did she ever learn to speak a word of English. Each of her children, however, spoke to her in English, while she would answer in her Indian language. Her body is also interred at Fairview Cemetery, beside her husband.

Unnamed members of the Rooks family, Pine Ridge, 1917.

On the Rooks family ranch, Pine Ridge, 1912.

From left: William, Charlie, Hobart and Eugene Rooks
at Pine Ridge

A great many offspring survive, among them 90-year-old William (Bill) Rooks. "I was number 10 of 12 kids in my family. My mother's mother adopted me. She took me away from Pine Ridge when I was about 3, but I remember how I was always starved." Asking what foods they lived on during the "lean years," he said they'd look for the vegetables and fruits growing wild. There'd be beans and wild turnips.

"Mother raised vegetables in her garden, too; you know, carrots and we had corn and peas, but mostly corn. She'd dry it and it would keep all winter. But when she'd cook it, it had to cook for a long time to get soft enough to eat.

"Once in a while they'd butcher a yearling. They cut the meat in strips and dried it in the open and then they stored it. It was like jerky.

"The fruit was good. There were chokecherries and the way they were prepared was to mash them, seeds and all, and then make patties. We had a flat roof on our house and the patties were put on the roof to dry but you had to watch out for the birds. The patties were good to eat but it was a lot of work to do," Bill remembered with a deep-seated sigh.

"Plums were great and grew wild. They were only about a half or three-quarters of an inch across the middle, but very sweet and delicious and they were made into a pudding." He added with a scowl, "The buffalo berries were good, too, and had a natural pectin, but those big trees they grew on were loaded with thorns and we'd get all cut up picking the berries. Besides that," Bill graveled, "we had to look out for the rattlesnakes, and there were gophers and other things."

As a youngster he was quite sickly, and he tells of being a lad when TB ran rampant through the reservation. "Half of the Indians had it," he spoke sharply, "and my brother was sent to a TB asylum, as they used to call the institutions, in Arizona to be treated for a year. They gave him a leave for a month and he came back to Pine Ridge. They sent me back to Arizona with him. My sister got the money for the transportation from the Bureau of Indian Affairs."

Bill's voice took on a special sparkle as he recalled his arrival in Arizona. "It was like heaven. It was wonderful there. They had pretty trees, and oleander and fields of roses. Holy gee, it was paradise. I stayed there in Phoenix and went to Indian high school, which I finished in 1939.

"In 1940 someone talked me into enlisting in the Air Force at Pine Ridge. They took us in a school bus to Cheyenne, Wyoming. They were going to send me to boot camp, but I had already been in the National Guard for two and a half years, so I was sent to St. Louis before going to Charleston. And then came Pearl Harbor Day!"

With great pride Bill tells of his years in the U.S. Air Force, stationed a while near New York City. In June 1942 the famous Flying Tigers were in China. The 14th Air Force was already there and took over the Flying Tigers airplanes, the courageous Colonel Pappy Boyington already having made a name for himself. Gregory (Pappy) in fact had won the Navy Cross as well as the Medal of Honor.

Bill Rooks was one of the AVG (American Volunteer Group), along with Pappy and stated, "I was the crew chief on one of the planes. Later they got us better planes made in England, the F51s." He continued, "I had a great life in China; never a dull moment. I spent 27 months there and was in the Air Force five and a half years.

"At the time of my discharge China was losing the war. Not the World War. The war against Communism. I was discharged on May 5, 1945. A couple months later," he sadly interjected, "the communists took over. Chang Kai-shek and others had to leave for Taiwan."

With Bill there was never a grain of regret, self-pity or annoyance with any hardships in his life. Always totally upbeat, he loved to remind people with great emphasis, "I never regretted anything about my life."

To digress, and more clearly explain the problems of the Native American Indians versus the U.S. Government, let's revert to ten years after Louis Bruce and Nellie's birth.

American Indians were introduced (in 1887) to the white culture with the Dawes Act. There was legislation which said all Indian tribal lands become private property. It had been thought that tribal culture kept the Indian people from becoming "civilized." Under this new Act an Indian family was given 160 acres, or 80 acres to individuals. This was to be held in trust for 25 years, theoretically keeping it secure from any white man who might somehow take it away from them.

While the theory appears sound, it did not work out as planned, for it had not totaled the amount of acreage allotted. Spotted throughout the area were pockets of land available to the white settlers. While it was unintentional, it left the Indian with less land than they had previously occupied. At the time of the Act in 1857 Indians held 138 million acres. By 1900 they were left with only 78 million acres, and were continuously dropped until in 1934 they were down to 48 million. Worse, the land allotted them was far less valuable, not meeting the needs of the Indians for their grazing cattle, farming or other requirements.

As stated in the book *Native American Indians in Early Photographs* by Tom Robotham, "The government seemed hell-bent on destroying Indian culture and showed little sign of improving living conditions."

Through countless centuries the nomadic Sioux followed the buffalo, their main sustenance. It fed and clothed them, as well as offered shelter. Tepees were of prime importance; this housing could be taken down and literally dragged to different homesites when a new location was essential.

Creation of tepees of the Plains Indians was unique. Three or four of the longest wooden poles available were wedged deeply into the earth at angles to form a conical shape. An additional hoisting pole was used to raise the tepee but was left lying on the ground. Guy wires were fastened to the top. A stake would be anchored in the center of the tepee with a rope securely tied to one of the posts, hopefully assuring it would stand up to any storm. These tepees were covered with carefully prepared buffalo skins, or, on occasion, with bark. When it became necessary to move their campsites, the structures could rather easily be taken down, rolled up and dragged to the next site.

It was generally felt that the winds blew from the west; consequently their doors always faced the rising sun of the east. It could take as many as a dozen skins to cover a tepee. In inclement weather an additional skin would be placed over the door for added warmth, as well as around the perimeter of the tepee.

Skins were also used to cover the ground for sleeping, as well as cut and sewn into their moccasins, loincloths and other clothing. The skins would first be soaked in ash and water. They would have to laboriously scrape the skins to rid them of the hair. Once the hairs were removed they would scour the skins for many hours with buffalo brains. Finally the skin would be smoked, and the arduous work would pay off, leaving it soft and supple. Before the age of steel tools, the Indians crafted their own implements from animal bones.

Frequently these Indians would paint and decorate their new tepees by using the juices of berries.

While parents were occupied with copious chores, youngsters could be seen playing with bows and arrows until they grew old enough and capable of joining their elders on hunting trips. Little girls loved their dolls, and most kids grew very agile by running around in fun and games.

In winter the lucky youngsters had sleds craftily created for them of wood, and often with bison ribs, sewn together with rawhide. These sleds were tremendously smooth-running across the winter snows and some say better than today's traditional sleds. Others played games on iced-over rivers. Once in a while there was someone good at sleight-of-hand to amuse friends. And there were simple games for elderly women who could sit in their tepees and play catch with small items.

The year 1904 was certainly an exceedingly important time in the lives of the happy bridal couple, Louis and Nellie Bruce. They honeymooned on a trip to New York City. After his 1904 graduation from dental school he practiced that profession for two years.

In 1905 they moved to Syracuse and lived on South Salina St. for two years. During this time their son Louis Rooks Bruce was born. In 1907 a little sister, Noresta Pamela Bruce arrived at this same address. It was then that Louis chose to give up dentistry and moved that same year to Onondaga Reservation where he found work at Smith's Typewriter plant. There was a trolley which could get him to his place of employment, but he had to walk three miles to reach that transportation.

It was in 1908 when Louis joined the Methodist Church where the Rev. John S. Miller was the pastor. In 1909 the Rev. George Moxey was pastor on the Onondaga Reservation and urged Louis to take a local preacher's course. He obliged by attending Syracuse University for three years. In 1910 he became pastor of the Methodist Reservation Indian Mission.

Pastor Louis found his new life very interesting with numerous organizations such as Women's Society of Christian Service, The Ladies Aid making and selling quilts in surrounding communities with profits going to the needy, occasional bazaars held in the church basement, Temperance Hall or the school across the road. The Epworth League for youths was very active and required his constant attention while he was also getting accustomed to superstitions and tribal contacts.

There were quite a few musicians in the community so they were able to form a male quartet to entertain in nearby towns and a popular trio of two very talented girls and a boy.

All this was most encouraging to Louis until fire struck and they lost the use of both the school and cottage. The pastor later wrote in his ledger that he was thankful for the large parsonage. It had accommodated not only his family but the four school teachers, the principal, his wife and their son.

Classes were held in Temperance Hall and the church until a dwelling was made available while the school and cottage were rebuilt. Meanwhile weekly prayer meetings were being held in individual homes. Parish life continued without a hitch.

Mrs. Bruce played the organ in the Episcopal Church but their son and daughter went to church with their father. That didn't work out too well, so Mrs. Bruce joined the Methodist Church too.

Many gifts of rabbits, wild ducks, pheasants, and woodchucks, with instructions on how to cook it, and even locusts fried in butter were given to the family.

The teachers and principal served as Sunday school teachers. And Mr. Bruce was proud to be able to get entertainers from Syracuse to come every so often through the year.

Cultural differences had to be respected to get along with the Onondagas. Whenever a child died, one of the chiefs walked from one end of the reservation to the other giving a "death whoop," (a shrill frightening yell). And of course whenever anyone died there was a wake. Hymns were sung, there were prayers and plenty of eats. A person, or sometimes a whole group, was awake all night. The Pagans believed that those who had died should have fresh fruit on their graves.

In 1911 a beautiful young wife of Isaac Lyons, famous Carlisle football star, was driven almost to desperation. Shunned by friends and relatives, she had been accused of being a witch with claims she had brought upon her husband the illness which kept him in the Hospital of the Good Shepherd in Syracuse.

Some of the Indians had inveigled Lillian Bigknife into drinking poisonous liquids and eating tainted food. They had wished her to die before her husband, in accordance with tribal custom thousands of years old. Every man, woman and child was bound to participate, each in his own way.

As the days wore on she grew more violent. The tribal people finally decided to break the spell they felt she held over her husband by throwing a still more powerful spell over her.

She was tricked into unburdening herself to an old woman who pretended to befriend her. Giving Lillian a strong amber-colored liquid which she quickly downed, the girl returned home, dazed and muttering incoherently.

After regaining her senses she repeated over and over, "I don't think there are any witches, but they're never going to get me." After everyone in her household fell soundly asleep, she stole into the woods, remaining in seclusion for a couple days and nights.

Early on a Saturday morning she appeared at the parsonage of the First Methodist Episcopal Church and asked Rev. Louis Bruce to pray for her. Her clothes were torn from thickets, her face and hair were covered with blood and there were unmistakable teeth marks on her wrists.

Rev. Bruce invited her in to rest. Later she explained to him that a figure had beckoned her into the woods, following her around.

On Sunday, October 1, 1911 The Washington Post reported that Louis Bruce testified that her condition was drug-induced. He felt it was apparent that the persecution had affected her mind and that the liquid given her had aggravated her condition. He said, "I have made quite an extensive study of narcotics and anesthetics because in my position I am frequently called upon to act as physician in the absence of better medical attendance. I'm quite sure that she had been given a drug of some kind. Her hands were cold and her head was covered with perspiration. Her pulse was very strong at times, and at times very weak."

In the long run, the court made no further investigation, and none ordered by the Indian authorities. Sadly, she lived the rest of her life on the reservation, but an outcast, condemned by all.

The Indians have large quantities of drugs and powders, some of which are poisonous and some so subtle that they baffle the expert chemists.

Rev. Bruce's memoirs speak of New Year's Day when traditionally, "A group of people, all ages, went to many houses carrying pillowcases and yelling *Happy New Year*. Each home gave cookies, candy or doughnuts, and then they went on their way."

The yellowed ledger continues to read, "Halloween was a spooky and mischievous event. A group of older boys would take off the metal gates from across the front of the church and parsonage lawn. They'd put them on top of the telephone wires. There were two double gates and two small gates.

"One particular Halloween Mr. Bruce decided to do something about this. There were six of these boys in the group. They had taken off all of the gates when Mr. Bruce appeared. Tapping a good six-footer on the shoulder, he said, 'Put those gates back on.' They didn't seem to hear so he repeated loudly, 'Put those gates back on, I said.' They immediately put them back. Any one of them could have knocked Mr. Bruce out with one punch."

Iva Gage told the incident of some drunken Onondagas creating a disturbance in the trolley. Mr. Bruce went over and told them to be quiet or they would be put off the car. One of them was a tall, robust man; anyway they quieted down in a hurry.

An addition to this same ledger continues with notes from 1917 to 1928, which follows, in part:

"His relatives from the St. Regis Reservation urged him to work among his people. He was transferred to Hogansburg in the Northern New York Conference. While here he fought the liquor problem among his own people, and urged them to become citizens of the U.S."

Sometime between 1917 and 1928 he built a beautiful stone church with the help of his son, Louis. On each of the two Indian reservations he had formed a male quartet.

It was also during his stay at Hogansburg that he was asked to get a group together to take to Columbus, Ohio to a Sesquicentennial. He wrote, "Twelve were from Hogansburg and one from the Onondaga reservation. They were to wear costumes and take basketry to display, to make and to sell. There were representatives from all over the world, in costume, and showing all kinds of articles. It was a real privilege to attend such a huge gathering."

While at Hogansburg several had known of Mr. Bruce being a dentist. Whenever anyone had a toothache they came to him. He hadn't kept up his license so he couldn't give any anesthetic, but that didn't make any difference to them. One day Noresta boiled the instruments, set a chair near a good window and put a pail beside the chair. When the patient was seated, Mrs. Bruce, Louis Jr. and little Noresta took a walk down to the riverbank. When they heard a loud holler they knew it was alright to come back inside.

Mr. Bruce couldn't speak or understand the Indian language and once in a while someone would come to the door, speak Indian to him, and he would say, "Would you like your tooth pulled?" They understood and would laugh and say, "No."

In the '20s Mrs. Bruce became an active member in the Eastern Star. They were asked to stay there in that city and were offered a home.

In her youth Noresta had been a student for ten years at the Government Indian School. Only after graduation did she study music and nursing. Noresta was a deeply religious person, cultured, talented and extremely well liked. Because of her proficiency in music she was able to organize choirs, quartets and duets. During the Centenary the Indian Male Quartet toured the North Country and she felt privileged to be their accompanist.

Another of her particular delights was to work with the youth in Sunday School. She and her husband made great partners through the eighteen years they served in the Onondaga and the St. Regis Indian Missions. Her beautiful spirit followed her throughout their lives.

In 1928 he made what must have been a very difficult decision, to try to get away from Indian work. He moved with his family to Evans Mills, N.Y. where, fortunately, it was very easy for the couple to make many new friends. A Men's Brotherhood was started. A great emphasis was put on a choir, and also a men's quartet. Union services were held between the Presbyterians, Methodists and Episcopal Churches. Besides that Evans Mills charge, he also had one at Pamelia, N.Y.

In 1937 he started preaching in Plessis and also at Redwood, N.Y. and the Oxford Group was flourishing. While at Plessis their daughter Noresta and Dorwyn Cable of Pamelia were married. The wedding took place in the parsonage,

Pastor Louis Bruce also preached at Depeauville and Stone Mills, N.Y. in 1940. Sadly, his precious wife was taken very ill in that same year and became an invalid for four years. Her daughter, a graduate nurse, took exceedingly good care of her for the duration of her illness. Through it all, she remained very cheerful and happy.

One bright morning in August of 1943 the much loved, beautiful Noresta Bruce was resting in her room, joined by her family. Her adorable little grandson Wayne was asleep in an adjoining room. Her husband was reading aloud Psalm 121, "I will lift up mine eyes unto the hills." Mrs. Bruce slowly opened her eyes, and then just as slowly closed them — forever.

Dorwyn Cable joined the military in 1944 and his wife moved in with her father. Little Wayne had been born on June 12, 1943 just two months prior to his grandmother's passing. There seemed no further desire for Pastor Louis to live in the North Country. When the next Conference came up, so did the opportunity to move to Columbia, three miles to the south of Ilion, N.Y. where he became pastor of N. Columbia, Columbia Center, So. Ilion and Cedar Lake.

Pastor Bruce found his five years covering these churches extremely rewarding. All of his family decided that was where they would like to permanently live. His daughter and her husband bought a home, requesting him to live with them.

Pastor Bruce retired in 1949, continuing to sing in the choir and make himself useful, doing little odd jobs around the church, keeping it neat and clean.

From 1954-1957 he preached in Nobleton, Florida during winter months, driving there by himself. After that he made the decision to remain home, keeping in contact with friends from school and baseball days through correspondence. Contentment also came from reading, but more so from watching his great granddaughter Angela Dawn Cable play on the back lawn and spending time with him each day. The family even took him along on their camping trips, which he enjoyed tremendously.

Louis Bruce suffered an illness which lasted three and a half years, and succumbed on February 9, 1968. Interestingly, the Superintendent of the Mohawk District was in charge of the funeral service. It was held at the Columbia Church with burial in Lake View Cemetery in Richfield Springs, N.Y. This ennobling Mohawk had risen to the occasion, lighting the pathways of countless numbers of his peers by his courageous deeds. Family and friends remember him reverently and with a hefty degree of awe.

Rev. Louis Bruce in his later years.

Wounded Knee and the "Trail of Tears"

I f we truly learn from our mistakes, it should follow that one of our great lessons should come from the horrific tragedies, the withering injustices, of The Trail of Tears and of Wounded Knee.

Much has been written and recorded on film about these devastating events. Our desire is not to belabor the issues but rather to try to be ever mindful of our mistakes and their bitter consequences.

For a millennium the Native Americans had successfully learned to live with those entities with which Mother Nature had endowed them. They deeply revered nature. They valued the spirits living within. Then came the Europeans who managed to usurp their lands. The Cherokee lived in Western Georgia and were anything but nomads. They were, in fact, farmers and ranchers. In 1830 the U.S. Congress passed the "Indian Removal Act."

We all recall Davy Crockett from the movies. It was he who was fervently against the Act, arguing with President Andrew Jackson against the unprecedented process of physically moving the Indians from their homes and livelihood, and all they knew and were comfortable with. In spite of the protestations the Act was passed. The Cherokees claimed to be a sovereign nation and took their case to the Supreme Court. It was a complicated issue and took some years to ponder. By 1832 Chief Justice John Marshall ruled that they were indeed a sovereign nation. Unfortunately the Cherokee were divided in their thinking.

The outcome was bleak. An abbreviated version of the years of wrangling was that Removal Companies were hired to escort the Cherokee men, women and children, plus other tribes, to be escorted by the military. They were to buy food for the Indians with chits authorized by the government. Uprooted from their homes and farms, these hapless people were herded into makeshift forts with minimal facilities and scant food. They were then forced to march a thousand miles to Oklahoma, through the harsh fall and bitter winter of 1838. Roughly 4000 to 5000 Creek Indians, plus thousands more from other tribes, succumbed to the brutality of this "Trail of Tears."

Of equal viciousness is the bloody event at Wounded Knee. Bill Rooks, a Sioux, originally from Pine Ridge, South Dakota, recalls all too clearly the stories of his mother and unschooled grandmother. Wounded Knee is on the Pine Ridge reservation, which covers 4,353 square miles (twice the size of Delaware). Somebody once said of Pine Ridge, "It's a place where nothing happens but the weather, and everybody waits for yesterday."

Bill Rooks readily stated, "Wounded Knee was a fall-out from Custer's Last Stand. In the Indian wars some of the men would take care of the other folks. At Little Big Horn there is a narrow valley which is good for hiding. It was here that Indian warriors took women and children to hide them. Grandma told me that Custer was a very foolish man. He was warned.

His troops were only 300 and the Indians were about 10,000 warriors. Grandma did not witness that fight but his whole regiment was wiped out. The Indian warriors also took all of the soldiers' horses. Grandma said that, 'In the beginning Custer thought he was going to wipe out all of the Indians.' Before the onslaught General Custer had divided his troops into three divisions. He and his regiment of 197 were killed at Wounded Knee.' "

In 1890 the U.S. Government failed to meet their obligations to the Sioux, such as the payment for sales of some Indian lands. Sadly their crops failed, too, and the government had cut back on supplies promised to them. Sitting Bull and his very hungry group formed a conspiracy, planning an uprising the following spring.

However, there are accounts of the "cult" of the Ghost Dance. By September it had spread through the Sioux Reservations in the hope for a new and better life ahead for the Indians, and their prayers for the restoration of the nearly extinct buffalo. In a manner of speaking the buffalo was the lifeblood of the Plains Indian. Although the Ghost Dance and the reasoning behind it were non-violent, the white men watching it were terrified. Consequently many Indians were arrested, and U.S. soldiers killed their beloved Chief Sitting Bull.

Big Foot learned of Sitting Bull's death and was fearful for his people. He and a group went up to Pine Ridge Reservation searching for a safe haven under Red Cloud, but they never made it. It is said that Red Cloud had raised a white flag of surrender when they rode up toward Government soldiers.

Bill Rooks' mother was 15 or 16 at the time of the infamous massacre which followed at Wounded Knee, December 28, 1890. She happened to be attending boarding school at Pine Ridge, approximately 15 miles away. She sadly recalls, "The soldiers attacked the Indians but first they disarmed all of them – except one Indian. He managed to slip into a tent. When the others had surrendered their rifles, they were lined up. The Indian inside the tent then fired through it. That's when the troops opened fire."

In recalling his parent's stories, Bill continued, "My mother said a bit later the Indians fired on the school, but from some distance and nobody was hurt. It appeared nobody was in charge." The school's occupants were, nonetheless, very frightened and hid under desks. The Indians had just gone wild. "Mother always remembered those scary things," he said, pityingly.

Birds-eye view of the battlefield at Wounded Knee, S.D.
Photo courtesy of and copyrighted by the Oglala Lakota College,
490 Piya Wiconi Road, Kyle, SD 57752.

Others have told of shots ringing out and the troops shooting indiscriminately, killing or wounding men, women, children and infants. Even today written accounts of the few survivors are bone chilling, the callousness of the drama beyond comprehension. The clothing which the Indians wore, thinking it would protect them, did nothing to help and 300 people lay strewn on bloody fields, ravine and stream, powerless to protect the helpless beings.

This was not only the needless death of Indian families and American troops, but also the end of the American frontier, the last fight between U.S. soldiers and the Native Americans.

Survivors reported that soldiers took moccasins and other souvenirs from the dead Indians.
Photo courtesy of and copyrighted by the Oglala Lakota College, 490 Piya Wiconi Road, Kyle, SD 57752.

Yet another version of the day's events is that of a newspaperman sent there from New York. He recalled that Indians were squatting or sitting in front of Big Foot's tent. The reporter strolled between the soldiers and Indians, attempting to jot down as much as he could of the happenings of the moment. He told his family later that there were a couple other reporters, a priest and an interpreter who was a mixed-blood Sioux named Bill Wells.

They were told that Big Foot was sick with pneumonia, lying in his tent. They brought him out and laid him on some blankets so that those in command could talk to him. The Indians had on what they thought were bulletproof "ghost" shirts. The reporter thought the Indians at that point were pretty sullen and defiant. As they were talking through the interpreter, the reporter said everything seemed to happen at once.

"The medicine men had just begun to throw handfuls of dirt into the air when a big Indian came charging out of a tent, yelling and brandishing a butcher knife." It was said he made a pass at the interpreter and cut off a piece of his nose. The interpreter grabbed his nose in his hand and put it back on.

At the same time a soldier tried to see if there was a gun under the blanket. The Indian shot the soldier in the belly. Another soldier slashed through a tent looking for hidden weapons. He was mowed down. The reporters, priest and interpreter had quickly hit the ground. Everything had broken loose.

The report was that Big Foot had probably been the first to die. Indians and soldiers who were close to each other engaged in hand to hand combat, while the other soldiers opened fire with their Hotchkiss guns, killing perhaps as many of their own men as they did Indians. As the Indians realized their "ghost" shirts were not protecting them, they ran for safety, the blood-crazed soldiers after them.

Clearer insight is shown in the following excerpt from Laurence M. Hauptman's book, *The Iroquois & The New Deal.* (Reprinted with permission of *Syracuse University Press*, Syracuse, N.Y.).

The issue here at Wounded Knee is the recognition of the treaties between the United States Government and the sovereign nations...

Sovereignty is freedom of a people to act and conduct affairs of its own nation. We, the Hotinonson, the Six Nations, have our sovereignty. We conduct on our territories and we act for our people. And so we have the Oglala Sioux which should conduct their affairs here because this is their territory, but who now have its government interfered with and who now have another form from another power acting within their territory.

Chief Oren Lyons (Onondaga)
Voices From Wounded Knee

[Note: Professor Hauptman is State University of New York Distinguished Professor of History, New Paltz, NY. He has authored many books on the Iroquois, winning awards for his distinguished service in his research and writings on American Indians.]

Gathering the bodies after the Battle of Wounded Knee, S.D.
Photo courtesy of and copyrighted by the Oglala Lakota College,
490 Piya Wiconi Road, Kyle, SD 57752.

Education, Pole Vaulting and The Great Depression

L et us now revert back to 1905, to the time of Louis Rooks Bruce's birth December 30th on South Salina St., Syracuse, at the edge of the Onondaga Reservation. He grew up, however, on the St. Regis Mohawk Reservation.

His father did a supreme job of paving the way for his education, making certain he attended private schools and had the opportunity to meet interesting people at every possible juncture. He attended Cazenovia Seminary but felt very uncomfortable as the only Native American student. Having to work his way through high school, and later through college, he became even more self-conscious. He was a farmhand, construction worker, paper mill worker, as well as a waiter. Perhaps being the lone Indian in a white man's world helped him excel in sports. He became captain of many teams in high school. In spite of all this he continued to feel inferior, deciding to major in psychology. He earned his B.A. from Syracuse University in 1930.

On November 19, 1930 he married Anna Jennings Wikoff. Anna was the daughter of Charles Wikoff, an attorney, and Kathryn Jennings Wikoff. Anna was raised and educated in Richfield Springs before furthering her education at Cazenovia Seminary where the couple became friends, and graduating from Syracuse University. Theirs was a loving and devoted relationship

The Bruce family: Noresta, daughter Noresta, Louis Sr. and young Louis Rooks Bruce.

There was more than a bounce in the heart and a spring in the step of Louis; there was a resounding jump. Louis loved pole vaulting, and the people who competed against or watched him loved it, too. Witness a few of the letters he had received.

406 Cambridge St.
Boston, Mass

Mr. Louis R. Bruce
Richfield Springs, NY

Dear Mr. Bruce:

You probably will wonder who I am, unless you remember, and why the letter, but I have never ceased to forget your most unfortunate mishap while practicing for the Semi-Final Olympic tryout here in Cambridge.

I still feel sure that you would have won out here against Brown of Yale and there is little doubt in my mind but that you would have been one of the three to represent the U.S. in the Olympics. Your exhibition in the Harvard indoor pit when you cleared 13 ft. 7 inches just before you fell showed perfect form. Dr. Gilbert Horrax of Williams College, who assisted me in the pole vault event, conceded first place to you over Sturdy and Brown.

It was my great honor to be elected President of the Boston Athletic Association for the ensuing year. In that capacity I take pleasure in sending to you under separate package a small charm as complements of the Boston A.A. for the mythical first place for which I think you deserved in that Meet. Kindly let me know whether you receive the package or not.

If it is going to be at all possible, I would like to have you entered in the New England A.A.U. Meet scheduled for the middle of February in the Harvard gym. We would like to have you compete under the Boston A.A. and your expenses taken care of by us in that event. Also an invitation to join the club is open to you. We can talk that over later if you are interested. Let me know if you would be interested in this coming Meet so that I can arrange for permission from your A.A.U. District.

I trust that you are keeping up your workouts for you ought to have an excellent chance in the next Olympics in Germany, and we would like to help you accomplish this aim. Good luck to you, and I would like to hear from you. I am,

Very truly yours,
/s/ Marc S. Wright
President of Boston A.A.

66 Cambridge St.
Boston, Mass.
September 26, 1933

Mr. Louis R. Bruce
Richfield Springs, New York

Dear Mr. Bruce:

I was very sorry to hear of your accident in pole vaulting during a Track Meet. Since August 1st, I have been out in the West coast and on my return saw an article in the New Times concerning the outstanding vaulters of the country and rating you as second best to Brown the record holder. Also stating the fact that your injury would prevent you from competing in the Meet this weekend in New York.

At a recent meeting held at Boston, of all the members of the Club, it was unanimously decided by vote, that you are to Captain the team on its trips, which also means that you will be in charge of the Team. We have scheduled a number of Meets but the outstanding trip will be the one to Oxford University, England around the 1st of June. Your progress in pole-vaulting during the past year has been very remarkable, discussed as being the most outstanding of any. I do want you to let us know at once your condition for we are naturally very much interested in our Captain. This election means that you may be required to move to Boston to serve as a full resident of the Club.

To me it was a very great joy to have you as Captain for it has been a pleasure to work with you and your influence and strong character has won you praise, not only in Track but also in the outer world to those who know you. Your personality has won you many friends wherever we have sent you to compete for we have had reports from others who know you, which certainly helps our Club.

Let me congratulate you on your success and I feel that, discarding accidents and injuries, you ought to be the coming World's Champion and we will help you to accomplish this end. Please let us know at once what your plans are and your physical condition. Go to it and you have my

Very best wishes for a successful year. I am,

> Sincerely
> /s/ Marc S. Wright
> President of Boston A.A.

From the other end of the continent Louis received the following invitation. His unique style and form had certainly not gone unnoticed.

> 620 W. 75th St.
> Los Angeles, California
> December 30, 1933

Mr. Louis R. Bruce
3715 93rd St.
Jackson Heights, L. I.

Dear Mr. Bruce:

Your competition in Amateur Track Meets in the East during the last three years and your success in the pole vaulting has won for you the honor of being second best to the record holder. Hence, it probably is your ambition to become the champion, and for this reason I am writing you personally, extending to you an invitation to become a member of the Los Angeles Athletic Club. We feel that we can give you the necessary training to accomplish your aims, for we have with us the three Olympic Team vaulters, Graber, Miller and Jefferson as well as Sturdy who has competed against you and gives an excellent account of your form and style of vaulting.

We have received reports from the various Meets that you have competed in and we find that because of your personality, courteousness to other contestants in Meets and good sportsmanship, you have helped a great deal in the good name your Club at Boston now has in athletics. It is that type of men we like to have representing us and I believe that we can offer you a better proposition than you now have.

If you are interested, we would like to know what type of business you are interested in and what experience you have had in order for us to make a connection here. Your expenses would of course be taken care of by the Club, and if married the same would be true for her. Let me know as soon as possible and give details as to business preference. I trust that you will accept this offer for we would welcome your membership and you could help us in your style of vault, as well as the help we can give you. We have found that you are a consistent vaulter which is very unusual for the event.

I hope that we receive a favorable reply and wishing you success for the coming year. I am,

> Very truly yours,
> /s/ Martin S. Grove
> President of Los Angeles A.C.

Louis's love of pole vaulting remained, and he had become a possible candidate for the 1936 Olympics, however an accident prevented that from happening. In the meantime he continued to work on the farm of his father-in-law Charles Wikoff and his wheelchair bound mother-in-law. Although Charles Wikoff was a stern and rigid man, the two families were able to live and work together in peaceful harmony.

Those of us old enough to recall living through the Great Depression are perhaps wiser for the economically disastrous experiences, but find it difficult to accurately describe to younger generations the multitudinous horrors and chaos it inflicted on mankind. With the Depression came FDR's New Deal, the Works Progress Administration (WPA), and the Civilian Conservation Corps (CCC). Never forgotten are the threadbare clothes, and holes in our shoes and socks. Our parents opening doors of poorly stocked iceboxes for the hungry or homeless who came begging for morsels of any leftovers, and the endless bread lines; an era when finding a job, any job, was a fantasy, a dream, and finding money for the rent was a nightmare.

Broadway High School. Noresta Bruce, front row, 3rd from left; her brother Louis in white shirt, tie and jacket to the right of tall man in white shirt, near center in 2nd last row."

As with the rest of the country, the Indian community was not immune to these problems and likewise hit very hard during the Great Depression. The Meriam Report shows that 96% of Indians earned less than $200 per year. Neither did it help to have Indian schools of poor quality, poor diets, overcrowded Indian boarding schools with a lack of adequate quality personnel, poor medical care, and reports still persist on the harsh discipline which had prevailed in that era – and still do.

Louis eventually made his way to New York City where he was employed at Rogers Peet, a clothing store at Fifth Avenue and 41st Street. Here he started work as a salesman, quickly advancing to Department Manager. He also became a model, a perfect 38, equivalent to a women's size 8.

One fateful day he spotted the easily recognizable First Lady Eleanor Roosevelt entering the upscale shop, her customary shawl draped loosely over her shoulders. She was a familiar sight in this, her husband's favorite clothiers. Unique for that day and age, the 1930s, first ladies and presidential families were not encumbered by the current ever-present Secret Service. She was able to walk about and browse freely, easily accessible to those interested in a chat.

As Mrs. Roosevelt attempted to choose a new tie, Louis Bruce took the opportunity to speak with her about the plight of the American Indian and deplorable conditions on the reservations. Always absorbed with things of current interest to the nation, the First Lady invited Louis to dinner at the White House to further discuss the problems. Also in attendance at that dinner was Aubrey Williams, head of the National Youth Administration (NYA). Louis's mind always spun in many directions, a virtual vortex of Indian knowledge. It did not take very long after the initial meeting before he became actively engaged in the workings of the NYA. In fact, the greater part of Louis's life was spent developing deeper interests in Indian culture and traditions, especially with regard to young Indians. Because of this interest in youth he created the first National American Indian Youth Conference in Washington, D. C.

First Lady Eleanor Roosevelt made herself accessible to the public.

In March 1936 he was appointed by the New York State Governor, Herbert H. Lehman, as head of the NYA for the State of New York. The WPA, or Works Progress Administration was going strong. The *Hudson River Valley Review* in an article titled: "Eleanor Roosevelt and the American Indian; the Iroquois as a Case Study" by Laurence M. Hauptman wrote:

> The NYA Indian program in New York State was largely administered out of a community building constructed by Indian youth workers in the center of the Onondaga Indian Reservation. By 1939 the NYA Indian program designed 27-week work programs and employed 248 Iroquois youngsters. Every Iroquois reservation in the state was affected by the size and scope of the undertaking.

It is said that using his sales experience and being inspired by the New Deal programs which put 85,000 Indians to work on reservations, Louis contrived the idea to put Indian boys in summer camps through-out New England.

On June 28, 1937 an Act was approved *"To Establish a Civilian Conservation Corps and For Other Purposes, as Amended."*

President Franklin D. Roosevelt, center.

AN ACT

TO ESTABLISH A CIVILIAN CONSERVATION CORPS,

AND FOR OTHER PURPOSES, AS AMENDED.

BE IT ENACTED BY THE SENATE AND HOUSE OF REPRESENTATIVES OF THE UNITED STATES OF AMERICA IN CONGRESS ASSEMBLED, That there is hereby established the Civilian Conservation Corps, hereinafter called the Corps, for the purpose of providing employment, as well as vocational training, for youthful citizens of the United States who are unemployed and in need of employment, and to a limited extent as hereinafter set out, for war veterans and Indians, through the performance of development of the natural resources of the United States, its territorial and insular possessions: PROVIDED, That at least ten hours each week may be devoted to general educational and vocational training: PROVIDED, That the provisions of this Act shall continue.

Original Act approved June 28, 1937 – Public No. 163, 75th Congress, 1st Session (50 Stat. 319)

This Act was followed by a letter written by President Roosevelt which read:

Greetings from the President of the United States

I welcome the opportunity to extend a greeting to the men who constitute the Civilian Conservation Corps. It is my belief that what is being accomplished will conserve our national resources, create future national wealth and prove of moral and spiritual value, not only to those of you who are taking part, but to the rest of the country as well.

You young men who are enrolled in this work are to be congratulated. It is my honest conviction that what you are doing in the way of construction service will bring you, personally and individually, returns the value of which it is difficult to estimate.

Physically fit, as demonstrated by the examinations you took before entering the corps, the clean life and hard work, in which you are engaged, cannot fail to help your physical condition. You should emerge from this experience, strong and rugged and ready for entrance into the ranks of the industry, better equipped than before.

I want to congratulate you on the opportunity you have and to extend to you my appreciation for the hearty cooperation which you have given this movement, so vital a step in the nation's fight for progress, and to wish you a pleasant, wholesome and constructive stay in the CCC.

Franklin D. Roosevelt

Louis attended the North American Indian Conference at the University of Toronto in 1939 and he established a section for Indian welfare in the New York State Welfare Conference.

Louis Rooks Bruce, 1940

The 1940s kept him equally busy as he returned to politics in 1941 to represent Indians at a seminar sponsored by the Carnegie Endowment for International Peace. Meanwhile, in the 40s he also continued to work on two dairy farms inherited from his father-in-law with a total of 762 acres. With these chores he meshed the two "careers" and served as president of the district chapter of the New York Youth Council in 1943, as well as being active in many other local programs. He loved focusing on young people and worked with them in 4-H, Boy Scouts and his Methodist church.

He became Director of the Farm Bureau of Soil Conservation, the Dairymen's League, and the Onondaga County Rural Policy Committee. There was never ever a dull moment in the life of Louis Bruce. He consistently found himself in charge of organizations, including the Six Nations Association.

Louis enjoyed fatherhood; he's cuddling Kate and Charles.

People constantly sought his help, and it would appear it was either impossible or difficult to turn anyone down. He and his wife Anna had three children: Charles Wikoff Bruce born in 1937, Kathryn (Kate) Bruce Huxtable, born 1939 and Donald Kenneth Bruce, born 1945. Although young at the time, Don easily recalls his dad, proudly stating, "Father was the pillar of the people." He further explained, "Dad worked for Grandfather Wikoff who had completed Cornell Law School. There were always people coming around to see dad. He never seemed to have a minute to himself. Sometimes he felt like hiding behind the barn, but that wasn't his nature. He always gave of himself and tried to help others if he could."

Always close to his dad, Don reminisced, "At one time Dad was head of the Boy Scouts. He took me once to a jamboree in Cimarron, New Mexico. There I met Chief Jim Iron Cloud and my two cousins, Richard Yellow Boy and Paul Fast Horse. We couldn't speak their language and they hadn't learned English so we had to use sign language to speak to each other."

Louis Bruce received the Boy Scouts of America's coveted Silver Buffalo award in 1972.

Don enjoyed recalling the sights of old Richfield Springs and how it had once been lined with fancy hotels. Horse drawn carriages would lazily saunter down the roadways and a trolley came there from Fly Creek, and eventually it went to Cooperstown.

But referring to their farm, Don mentioned, "When Grandpa Wikoff got out of law school he made a tremendous success of the farm, raising sheep, cows, hops, sugar beets, and corn. The farm then consisted of 600 acres, 200 of which were across Lake Canadarago. The farmhouse was started in 1882, growing to a 22-room home, easily accommodating the indigent, sometimes drunken or orphaned youth, or those from broken homes. Louis dared to shelter the beleaguered, downtrodden Indian and occasionally white youth.

Stacks of grain drying in the warm sun; farmhouse in background.

And Grandpa Wikoff was just as persistent as his son-in-law, a very determined person. He hauled his own milk with a sleigh. He believed in the Amish theories and didn't want any mechanized things around the farm until after he died. Don has advised, "Grandpa would always ride his sleigh and kept a double-barreled shotgun next to him."

In the years when Don's father ran the farm, he'd see that the hundreds of cows had been milked and when endless chores could be put aside for the day, he'd make sure that the Indian boys would have time to play, preferably lacrosse in their sprawling fields. (His son Don still has his dad's old wooden lacrosse stick.) There was always a balance of work and play to the extent that it was feasible.

Richfield Springs, NY 22-room farmhouse; field in front used for playing sports. An exchange student from Germany was scratched on its barbed wire fence while playing.

Don is justly proud of his father and the fervor and passion, which spurred him through life. There were so many accomplishments, it's impossible to keep track of all of them.

In 1949 Gov. Dewey appointed him to the Board of Thomas Indian School. He also served as Chairman of the President's Advisory Committee on American Indian Affairs.

Freedom Foundation Award Winning Essay

I n 1949 Louis wrote an article carried in *The American* magazine and reprinted in the *Reader's Digest*. This earned him the Freedom Foundation Award, presented by General "Ike" Eisenhower for his contribution to "Americanism." A copy of the essay is enshrined in a time capsule at the base of the flag at the headquarters of the Freedom Foundation at Valley Forge. It is to be opened in the year 2049. With great pride it is reprinted here.

General Dwight D. Eisenhower (left) greets Freedom Foundation Award winners. Louis R. Bruce, extreme right.

Freedom Award, 1950. From left: J. Barret Scarborough, Publisher, *The American Magazine*; former President Herbert Hoover; Dr. Wilford I. King, prominent economist; Sou Chan, New York restaurateur; Louis R. Bruce, Jr. Director of the Dairymen's League's Youth Cooperative.

A Mohawk Indian tells
What America Means to Me

My father is, to my mind, the essence of good Americanism. Through his career he maintained that the opportunities of America are unlimited for any person, regardless of origin, who has the energy and persistence to pursue them. It was Dad who showed me the trail any Indian can take to become a successful, well-rounded citizen in an atomic age America.

Dad was a full-blooded Mohawk Indian. He was slated to become Chief of the Mohawks, as his father had been, but instead he chose to "leave the blanket." He became a Christian minister, and a baseball pitcher.

When I was a youngster I felt – like most Indians – pretty apprehensive because I was an Indian. I couldn't help but feel that I belonged to a persecuted underprivileged group. Dad kept telling me to stop being disturbed about the fact that I was an Indian. He said that in modern America everything would depend on what I made of myself, and that I would have just exactly as much opportunity as the next person. "Your obstacles," he kept saying, "are mainly in your own mind."

Today I know he is right. And I know that what he taught me about America made up the most valuable lessons of my life.

Many of America's 400,000 Indians haven't had the benefit of a pep talk from my dad and mother. They are still skeptical about their chances of getting ahead in a modern America. They feel that any person who is known to be an Indian is excluded from America's opportunities, and handicapped in many insuperable ways. Consequently, some of them are ashamed of their Indian heritage. They try to hide it,

The other day I was talking to a U.S. Congressman from a western state about Indian legislation. Suddenly he gave me some man-to-man advice.

"Bruce, you ought to know better than to go around admitting you're an Indian," he said. "You know as well as I do that most Indians are low-down good-for-nothing savages, and you will just mess up your business career if you identify yourself with them."

The interesting point of that story is that I happen to know the congressman himself is part Indian, though he has never publicly admitted it.

I am an Indian, all right, and am proud of it, thanks to my father and mother. I come from a long ancestral line of "aboriginal savages," as the textbooks phrase it. Not only was my dad a Mohawk, but my mother was a Sioux, a relative of Sitting Bull.

The Mohawks and Sioux, you may remember, resisted the white invasion of their native lands with ferocity and cunning. In fact, they probably made it hotter for the White Man than any other two tribes on the continent.

Today the White Man is paying me off for the lands he took from my ancestors. Each year I get two checks. My check from the Mohawk Annuity Fund this year came to $2.38. And my last annual check from the Sioux reservation in South Dakota was for $32. That covered the profits the reservation made on 160 acres of very poor grazing land allotted to me. The two checks keep me in chewing gum, one of the White Man's products I like very much.

My Indian name is Agwelias, which was given me by Grandfather Bruce. I was born and raised on New York reservations, and most of my relatives still live on reservations.

During my boyhood I heard a lot of bitter talk about the raw deal Indians have gotten in their native land. Although I had two swell white friends, Kenneth McKinnon and Bill Hamilton, in Hogansburg, I heard repeatedly from some neighboring whites that Indians were "no good trash." And I heard from Indians that it was hopeless for an Indian to "leave the blanket" and try to improve his position in America, because of deep prejudice against Indians.

Today I know better. And I don't have to look far to prove my point. I just go up on the hill at the farm. I was up there last night after I had finished milking. The reason I went up was that I wanted to think about this article, and I can think better up there.

From the hilltop I could look out over the breathtakingly beautiful Mohawk Valley of central New York, Nestled below at the edge of our property was Lake Canadarago (an old Mohawk name). Hundreds of years ago Mohawk Indians used to ccme down to the pasture by the lake. About a year ago my uncle dug up some old arrowheads down there. He found them near the old Indian mounds which scientists have come from Colgate University to examine. The road that winds down past our house, now Route 28, used to be an old Mohawk trail.

In the dusk last night I saw a line of animals trailing single file toward the old camping ground. They were our herd of heifers and milk cows going out to pasture, but for one chilling second I imagined they were Indian ponies.

For centuries before the White Man came to drive away the Mohawks these rolling hills were the happy hunting ground of my ancestors. Now they form the heart of the richest dairy country in North America. And I, an Indian, am able to call 450 acres of this land (or almost a square mile) my home.

From those cows in the pasture we drained many thousands of quarts of milk last year, as well as selling many calves. In addition to the cows, we have 600 chickens, 12 hogs, and 13 horses. Some people claim I'm old-fashioned to stick to horses instead of using tractors. But, being an Indian, I'm a sentimental fool about horses.

Except for the horses, however, we are fully mechanized, and our 22-room house has a streamlined, electrified kitchen. We raise every bit of our own grain. The farm has been called one of the "best worked" in Otsego County. Its market value, I've been told, would exceed $100,000.

As I stood on the hill last night I could see, farther down the lake, Richfield Springs, one of the finest communities in America. I am fortunate to be a member of the local Rotary, the Masons, the Grange. And until two months ago, I was superintendent of the Sunday school and I still am a trustee of the Methodist Church, whose spire I could see.

Also, from the hill, I saw the farms of my many wonderful neighbors; men who have helped me become an executive of the National Milk Producers Federation and of the Dairymen's League Co-operative Association.

At the age of 41 I believe I am as rich in friends as almost any American. And friendship is the only wealth that the average Indian values.

I don't wear a headdress but throughout my career I have always made it clear to people that I am an Indian, to prevent any possible embarrassment. And since I left the reservation I have invariably been treated as just another typical American guy, which is the way I like it. As I stood on the hill last night I felt pretty proud to be a citizen of modern America.

Most of America's 400,000 Indians today suffer from an enormous inferiority complex brought on by centuries of humiliation and callous treatment by the whites. Because of this inferiority feeling it is not easy to "leave the blanket" and "go the white way." It afflicted me too. I would still be on the reservation, if it were not for my dad, Awananeu, or Louis Bruce, Sr. (Almost all the older Mohawks and Onondagas still refer to me as "Little Louie.")

As a boy my father was sent to an Indian school in Philadelphia where he became a fervent convert to Christianity — and a baseball player.

One day, while he was pitching, a man by the name Cornelius McGillicuddy, who later became better known as Connie Mack, was deeply impressed by Dad's smoke ball. The upshot was that Dad was able to earn his way through college pitching for the Philadelphia Athletics and other teams.

Dad never went to the mound without spending a few minutes in prayer. A few years ago the Associated Press interviewed Ed Barrows, Yankee Manager, on Barrows' long career. The article said, "Though Babe Ruth and Honus Wagner were the greatest ballplayers he ever saw, Ed named an Indian as the greatest natural ball player of them all. 'His name is Louis Bruce,' said Ed."

Today Dad is 70 and a retired minister. Last Saturday I caught some of his pitches as I have for years. This may seem incredible, but I honestly believe his arm is in the best condition I've ever seen it. He had real steam, curves, and drops.

Dad quit pitching professionally when he became New York State's first Indian dentist. As a dentist he made good money, but he became imbued with a great thought. He wanted to go back to his Native Indians as a Christian Missionary. Only through Christianity, he felt, could they find the resources to become respected citizens of a modern America.

For 16 years he served as a missionary on the Onondaga and St. Regis reservations in upstate New York. Then he tackled a still greater challenge and became a Methodist minister to white congregations. He served successfully in Evans Mills, Depauville, Plessis, and North Columbia, N.Y., where he retired.

The great battle in Dad's life was for Indian citizenship, in 1924. Indians were wary. They thought citizenship was another white trick, to make them lose what little they felt they had left. Dad campaigned all the reservations in the state to build up support among Indians for U.S. citizenship. He argued that he was anxious to take responsibility for the kind of government we have in America, and the kind of schools we have for Indian children.

The happiest day of Dad's life was the day he and Mother were able to vote.

Dad felt no resentment whatever toward the whites. He recognized full well that a lot of injustice had been done to Indians, but he argued, "It's not going to help our progress to keep harping on old grievances. Instead, let's build for the future."

Mother and Dad were almost never well off financially. He rarely earned more than $600 a year during those early days of the ministry. Yet every summer Dad and Mother had "Fresh Air" youngsters out from New York City, kids of all nationalities, races and backgrounds. They wanted my sister Noresta and me to learn how to understand and get on with all the kinds of people you find in America.

Despite everything that Dad told me, I was still concerned about the future because I was an Indian. I still kept hearing on every side that Indians were lazy, good-for-nothing trash. When you kept hearing it day after day you began to say to yourself, "Look; you're one of them." I was obsessed by a really bad inferiority complex.

Dad decided to take drastic action — to throw me into the American stream of life and let me sink or swim. He arranged for me to go to Cazenovia Seminary, a Methodist school, where he could get me a reduction in tuition because he was a preacher.

The 300 boys and girls there had apparently never seen an Indian before. They expected me to say, "Ugh. Heap Big School" every time I opened my mouth. And they seemed greatly puzzled because I wasn't wearing buckskins. In a sense, my dress was unusual. I wore slacks and sweater rather than a suit, and we were supposed to wear suit coats in chapel and dining room.

During those first weeks at Cazenovia I was terribly conscious of being watched, not only by the students, but by my parents and the other Indians back at the reservation. (Many had predicted I would come out on my ear.) I felt like Jackie Robinson must have felt when he started playing for the Dodgers.

If I had failed that first test I'm not sure where I would have ended. Maybe I would have crawled back into my shell. Happily, the lessons my father had drilled into me about getting along with all kinds of people paid off. I became captain of Cazenovia's football, basketball and track teams, and became president of my senior class.

One role I had I shall never forget. I had the male lead in the Junior Play, and I played opposite the leading lady, a white girl named Ann ("Charlie") Wikoff. I tumbled for Ann and am still in love with her. Eventually she saw some merit in me.

She was the daughter of a wise, prosperous, Cornell-educated farmer, Charles Wikoff who, it turned out, was a prominent Methodist layman and an old friend of my father.

Ann and I went on to Syracuse University together. During several summers I earned my college tuition, or most of it, for the coming year by working as a hired man on her father's farm.

Each month at school was touch and go financially. I waited on table every single day that I was at both Cazenovia and Syracuse. I mowed lawns, dug postholes, cracked rock, wrassled logs at a paper pulp mill, operated a pick and shovel. I never saw a college football game, because I had to work Saturdays. And although I was Syracuse's star pole-vaulter I was never able to take an out-of-town trip with the team, because of my urgent need to make money.

Most Indians who have a chance shine in athletics, and I guess I was no exception. I never lost a major meet in high school. And today, at 41, I can pole-vault better than I could in college. I had a pole-vaulting pit by the barn. A few months ago I cleared 14 feet. The Olympic championship last year was won by a vault of 13 feet 8 inches. I mention this only because I know that having one outstanding skill played a big part in helping me overcome my haunting sense of inferiority.

At college I majored in psychology mainly to learn more about this inferiority complex that plagues my race. I found that it afflicts all sorts of people, not only Indians, and for all sorts of reasons. As I studied the psychology of typical Americans I concluded they are far more assertive, competitive and aggressive than Indians. I, like most Indians, tended to be diffident, reserved, close-mouthed. The hardest thing in the world for an Indian to do is to be aggressive, to put himself across. That's probably why so few Indians have ever attained notable success in business.

Whatever career I might select, I still felt a deep need to prove to myself that I could succeed vocationally in a typically American way. What is the talent Americans seem to admire most? What is the talent that sets them apart in the world? I decided it was salesmanship. Americans unquestionably are the greatest salesmen on earth.

So I set out, grimly, to become a salesman. I signed up for merchandising courses and got myself a spare-time job selling on commission at Peck & Vinney, a men's clothing store in Syracuse.

Each night I practiced putting myself across in front of my mirror. What a ridiculous Indian, I thought! Sometimes I felt like slinking back to the reservation. At the store, each customer looked like an unassailable monster. I would clench my fists and wade into him with my most practiced smile.

My Dad's training in getting on with all sorts of people came to my rescue again. When, in the third week, I managed to sell to a traveling salesman, who wanted "something around $35" a $60 suit, I decided that maybe even an Indian could learn to sell.

I wrote my final college thesis on "The Manufacture of Men's Clothing." In my research I visited the Stein-Bloch factories, corresponded with officials of Hart, Schaffner & Marx, and interviewed officers of the Hickey-Freeman Company.

Then I was graduated into the cold, cold world of 1930, year 11 of the Great Depression. College graduates were a nickel a dozen, not to mention Indians. When I finally heard that a big Rogers Peet store in New York City was hiring a salesman I borrowed train fare and hurried down. There were numerous applicants, many of them Harvard, Yale, and Princeton graduates. I got the job. Why? Because I knew the men's clothing business inside out, knew the lingo.

Ann, who was now my wife, came down and got a job selling women's sports wear at McCreery's. We managed to get along well in New York. Soon I became a department head with five assistants. I was headed up. But actually I wasn't enthusiastic about a business career. I was still too much of an Indian to be really interested in making money. I had gotten into selling to develop the peculiarly American talent of assertiveness.

What was much closer to my heart was the plight of hundreds of Indian youngsters back on the reservations. Perhaps I felt guilty. At any rate the Depression had frozen them out of contact with the white world. There were no jobs, and absolutely nothing to occupy them. They were drifting back to the reservation. In my visits I had found them demoralized and more ashamed than ever that they were Indians. Many fine boys I knew had become hoodlums.

Here was a challenge that fascinated me. But what to do? I got a clue one day from a customer. He was director of a boys' camp in the Adirondacks. When he learned I was an Indian he began telling me about his camp's big "Indian" program. It taught its youngsters Indian dancing, Indian legends, Indian ceremonials, archery, canoeing, tracking, Indian arts and crafts, mask-making.

Who taught the courses? I asked. "Oh, anybody," he replied. "We have some counselors who boned up on Indian stuff at the library. They're not so hot, but they're the best we can get."

Suddenly I was dazzled by a brainstorm. I couldn't sleep nights thinking about it. Every night after work I did research on camp programs. There were thousands of camps between Maine and Indiana that had "Indian" programs, but not a single one used real, live Indians.

I went to Indian chiefs back on the Onondaga reservation. They agreed that "Little Louie" had a wonderful idea! Their eyes blazed with excitement. But then they sighed. The trouble was that all the young Indians were not interested in their Indian background. And the elders had not been able to pass on to them Indian skills and lore. It would take at least a year to train them properly.

We were licked. As we sat gloomily in the tribal council house I came up with another idea: The Great White Father in Washington was then shoveling out billions of dollars for leaf-raking projects. Perhaps he could spare a few thousand to help get this started. The hunch was correct. I sold an agency director on the idea, and quit the Rogers Peet Company.

Soon I was putting my selling talents to work in persuading hundreds of summer camps to hire Indian counselors. Altogether, in five years, I helped put 600 Indian boys on camp staffs, where they made good money, where they came in contact with fine, educated white boys, and where they were able to feel proud of their Indian background.

It was a real inspiration to see these Indian boys come back from the camps, transformed by the experience. For the first time many felt they were Americans, not tolerated second-class citizens. Several hundred were inspired to resume their effort to get a high-school education. Many of them went on to college. Though federal funds were withdrawn long ago our New York reservations today are still supplying many camps with Indian counselors.

In 1940 I felt my job was done. Besides, both Ann and I were tired of traveling around and living in cities, because we now had two children. I felt a need to get out where I could sweat and use my muscles again. More important, I felt a yearning to get back to the land, to settle down in a small American community and sink roots.

I wanted to succeed in a typical American community, and in a way where I could feel I was rendering service to my fellow men, as my father had done all his life. For years I had wanted to become a farmer in a small farming community. To me the farmer is the most enviable man in the world. He has freedom, independence, and — like Indians — he lives in close harmony with nature.

So I began shopping for farms. One day, when Ann and I came back to the home of Ann's parents for Sunday dinner, Mr. Wikoff mentioned that he was getting along in years and was eager for an opportunity to withdraw gradually from active interest in his fine farm.

We bit hard. In a few days we made a deal with Mr. Wikoff. I was in the farming business.

In a few years I took on a 160-acre farm across the lake as an additional project. Since then I have bought and sold other property. Eventually I hope to have 150 head of cattle.

Ann and I were soon having the time of our lives getting into PTA, Boy Scouts, church work, and other community activities in Richfield Springs. I have a Sunday-school class of teen-age boys. With them, I suspect, my Indian background is an asset.

It wasn't long before I noticed that the young folks of Richfield Springs were up against much the same discouraging problem that faces Indian youngsters on the reservations. Richfield Springs had become a dead resort town. Many years ago it had 16 tourist trains daily and a flock of fine tourist hotels. But most of the tourists stopped coming. And the enterprising young people of town, facing a grim future, were starting to leave. There was nothing to hold them.

With the assistance of our school principal, Everitt Lane, and others, I got several of the young people who were left together. We began holding town meetings on the theme, "Does our town have a future?" You may have read in the newspapers about the results. The young people, with the backing of the village fathers, inspired many new ideas, and new industries were brought to Richfield Springs. Several youngsters have become top leaders in the community.

Meanwhile, as a farmer I became a member of the Dairymen's League Co-operative Association. Through the sponsorship of Dairymen's League Director and New York State

Assemblyman Paul Talbot, I was elected president of the Otsego County League. And with the support of Mr. Talbot and the members we developed an active youth program in the county.

Ann looks after things when I am away from the farm. We have four hired boys, including a talented Indian orphan. Also, we are teaching the two oldest of our three kids to shoulder responsibility for the farm. They have regular chores. Katie, 9, feeds the calves, drives the cows to pasture at night, gathers the eggs. Chuck, 12, throws down the hay, weeds beets, and does our hand milking. And Donnie, 3, runs errands to the best of his ability,

Katie is happy to be considered an Indian. But when people ask Chuck, he usually hesitates and says, "Nope, I'm not but my dad is."

Yes, I'm an Indian and I'm awfully proud of the recent accomplishments of my race. After a century of crushed humiliation as wards of a paternalistic U.S. Government, Indians today are demanding the right to have a voice in their own future as Americans.

I think it is wonderful that so many leading Indians today are impatient to guide their own destiny and "get things done." We are becoming competitively assertive in the best American sense. One spectacular result of this assertiveness is that we have formed a National Congress of American Indians, the first national all-Indian organization in American history.

Already we have 100,000 members. Each pays dues, and tribes are members as units. I am proud that I can put my selling ability to work by serving as the NCAI's unpaid legislative contact man in Washington and as a member of the executive committee. Also helpful in this cause is the fact that I am vice-chairman of Secretary Krug's National Advisory Committee on Indian Affairs.

Still more encouraging than this new assertiveness, I believe, is the fact that most young Indians today are really eager to become self-reliant. They will accept all the assistance they can get from group action, but they know that in the last analysis it will be up to each individual Indian to become a competent, responsible American citizen.

I hope and believe I have become a modern American citizen. My father is satisfied. Of that I'm proud. But I am even more proud that I am a modern American of Indian ancestry.

General Dwight D. Eisenhower presents Freedom Foundation award to Louis R. Bruce.

Making a Difference

L ittle Louie" had good reason to be proud. In many ways he "made a difference," at his farm, in his community, and helping his people across the entire nation. Louis had a heart of gold and a penchant for assisting the down trodden, the young Indian boys who succumbed to alcohol and caused grievous problems, either in school or on the reservations. Some were known to leave their embattled parents, go off to steal food from houses and hide away to eat and sleep, sometimes in haylofts or any place out of sight. Louis and Anne's heart and hands were always stretched out to aid and lead.

And there were those Indians across our land who disliked being torn from parents, sent to schools where they were shunned by the "white folk," and hated their life of misery. One such person was Jone Green, a Tuscarora girl. Jone grew up, eventually, to become a very productive, charming American citizen, an avid reader, painter and serious student of the Bible. But before that could take place she had to survive her youth, first through aforementioned forced schooling; next through the auspices and under the watchful eyes of Anna and Louis, and finally through college.

Kate, Don and Chuck at family farm, 1947.

As a youngster she had been sent from home to an Indian school in Oklahoma. Children had come there from all across the country but forbidden to speak their own languages. While it was interesting getting to know other kids from many tribes and learn of their cultural differences, Jone admitted it was nonetheless a difficult time and great strain for her and most of the others.

When she was able, she left Oklahoma for New York State and the Thomas School on the Tuscarora Reservation. While there she'd sadly walk each day to her classes, looking up at the building with a Biblical inscription from John emblazoned near the top of the wall. It seemed to speak aloud to this young girl; yet she wondered for a long time what the prophetic words really meant. Finally it came to sustain her, to give some meaning and as yet an unknown purpose to her life. *"You shall know the truth and the truth shall set you free."*

Getting to school meant marching (not walking) there to tolling school bells. "Everything was regimented," she scowled. "We couldn't speak our own language, either. It's all but forgotten." In many ways these youngsters were lucky to have been chosen and make it to school. For another thing, the infant mortality rate was very high on the reservations and you were lucky to reach school age. And then only certain children were chosen for an education.

Jone explained that breakfast at boarding school was nothing to look forward to. Oatmeal had been made into a watery gruel, but she quickly added with a glint in her dark eyes, "Sometimes when the Catholics left for church on Sunday the rest of the kids would have cold cereal, and *those corn flakes were most welcome.*"

The Thomas school was situated close enough to farmland which made fresh fruits and vegetables readily available in the summer months. There were juniper berries, huckleberries and blackberries. Jone frowned in her expressive way that you had to be especially careful when picking blackberries because they were also the bear's favorite dessert and you didn't want to become his main course.

Corn soup was a popular item and it took several processes to make it. "It was prepared in a big black kettle," Jone vividly recalled. "At times they would add kidney beans, and sometimes they might even have a little pork which would give it added flavor. Salt, however, was very hard to come by."

Her less than appetizing description was, "At school we would eat pig scraps. It would last all day; sometimes it would still have the hide on." Talk about not wasting a single thing!

"If we'd behave, we might even get a little money, maybe even a nickel.

"And we'd have to dress nicely when the Superintendent came. And if you got an A or sometimes even a B in deportment, you might get a nickel. But if you didn't get an A or B, you <u>still</u> had to walk up to the Superintendent, shake his hand, and say 'thank you' — even when you didn't get anything at all."

A smile swiftly crossed her pleasant face. "When the kids would spend their nickel they could get a small bag of popcorn or pretzels. They would find a place to sit down together, open their little paper bags and share their goodies with each other." These times were precious and few, but long remembered.

Sunday School each week was interesting for the girls. For one thing, they got to wear a different dress on that day. That was a really big deal! You felt a bit more vibrant, less drab. It was something to which they could look forward.

Jone stated somberly that the school staff was treated like royalty. She added, "They got the cream from the top of the milk while we got the old stuff." (Oh those days before homogenization.) "While they had set meals most days, we kids got the leftovers. We were always hungry, so we tried to help out in the bakery, if possible, because then maybe we could get some crumbs - or even a cookie! Wow!"

One of the vegetables Jone particularly recalled was lettuce prepared with sugar and vinegar. And that brought to mind their "epic Iroquois tale" of *the three sisters: corn, beans, and squash.*

Long ago the Iroquois received a message from The Peacemaker which is the basis for the Six Nations Iroquois Confederacy, The Great League of Peace. The Peacemaker ended all strife among the Iroquois in a series of laws recorded in belts of shell wampum beads. There are fifty chiefs, their duty being to maintain The Great Peace. The Peacemaker stood the fifty chiefs in a great circle, planting a tall pine tree in the center. They are to make sure it never falls.

And the Iroquois were given four plants. The sacred tobacco plant was used to communicate with the spirit world. The other plants, corn, beans and squash, were to sustain life. They were called The Three Sisters. It is said that at the time of Creation the Sky Woman carried the roots of these plants to the Turtle Island (North America), and they became the staple food of the Iroquois. The Iroquois believe that each plant has a female spirit.

Three Sisters: corn, beans and squash, from a carving. Photo courtesy Iroquois Indian Museum, Howes Cave, NY.

Jone recalled details as if it were yesterday. "If you were lucky you had a corn husk doll. And we learned songs, about a friend, and an Apache Sun Dance song. And there was another holy song we learned from the Mohawks." Singing it brought a far away look into deep eyes. Asking what it meant, she replied they had no idea, it was holy and so they did not know the meaning of the words.

Medicines, as in all cultures around the world, played an integral part of their lives. The Indians of this New York/Canadian region were far ahead of their time in many of these things. Cures were found long ago for scurvy and hypertension but the major problem was finding the proper dose of any medication for any given disease or ailment. People also misdiagnosed a patient's problems, thus often mistreating them, even when they knew the cure. (If you recall in telling how the Longhouses were constructed, the lad would be given the same "tea" for his cold by his grandmother as used in sealing the Longhouses. So just what would be a proper portion, not too poisonous to do grievous harm?)

Some examples of medicines would be the Trailing Arbutus which was found in New England. It was used for possible blood and kidney problems. Dried bark of the root of sassafras was used. One man had a badly injured arm and a poultice of sassafras was prepared and wrapped around the arm, curing it. Basswood was known to aid many ailments. Countless items are recorded in Indian annals.

A humorous Indian saying is: "Strawberries line the way to heaven." It therefore brought a chuckle when a gentleman, after a near collision, remarked, "I almost ate strawberries."

It was in 1953 that Jone had had it with school and was fortunate to have the Louis Bruce family invite her to stay at their farm in Richfield Springs, to help around the house. She was but one of a great many young boys and girls he befriended in this manner over a period of years. While work could be hard, these are the most cherished days in the life of Jone.

Don explained that his father was always rushed with countless tasks and meetings on the short visits to his home, his beloved farm. He had to rely heavily on his wife to run things. While the "hired help" could generally be relied upon, there were those with innate drinking problems. One such Indian lad would be awakened early each morning for his milking chores. When Anna Bruce could not hear the squeaking equipment she'd be off to the various haylofts to inevitably find her sleeping hired hand.

Grandpa Bruce in headdress showing his grandchildren numerous Indian artifacts. He was an avid collector. 1950.

"Mother ruled the roost," Don clearly remembered, but she was always good-natured about the silly little things young kids would do. Don was no saint either, and smilingly recalled his daily trips to the chicken coop as a youngster, plucking the eggs from their nestled berths among cackling hens. Not all of the eggs would make it to the kitchen. Instead some would be splattered on walls, people passing nearby, or anything in sight, as the whim moved him.

There were times when he, or other pranksters, paid for their fun by being dunked in the watering tank, normally kept for the cows.

Meantime Jone helped with many household chores, setting the dining room table, doing laundry, operating the mangle on bedding or clothes which needed ironing. Girls and boys had to do the cleaning. Jone learned to render fat for lard. There was an apple orchard on "Grandpa Wikoff's farm" as they often referred to it. She helped with baking pies, preparing applesauce and even made vinegar from apples. Jone remarked that, "Grandma would say 'get me some vinegar, but not the mother on the top of the vinegar.' And we would get watercress from down in the stream for our watercress sandwiches. We also canned Seckel pears. They were small but so very tasty. And they had a vineyard for our grapes, and all the things we made with them. Harvest time had everyone bustling about, outdoors and in the kitchen.

"There was one thing for sure, though. Neither Louis Bruce, father or son, would ever do any work on Sundays!"

Jone was very quick to advise, "Grandpa Wikoff' was awfully stern and always demanded hard work from everybody, but commanded the same of himself. He was also on the school board of Richfield Springs. Meanwhile Grandma Wikoff spent her spare time studying the Bible."

Regarding games or toys Jone remembers from childhood, a soft smile crossed her round face. She wistfully replied that there were jump ropes, jacks and tidily-winks. She embraced the thought that Indians fought in all the U.S. wars, but regrets they were invariably segregated from the other soldiers.

After a couple glorious years in their fold, Jone left the Wikoff/Bruce farm for college in Albany, while remaining ever mindful of the goodness and tender care of the Bruce family. They shall all forever live in her heart.

Louis's interest in youth never waned and he created the first National American Indian Youth Conference in Washington, D.C. in 1957. His founding the National Congress of American Indians and serving as Chairman of the President's Advisory Committee followed this on American Indian Affairs.

APR 13 1950

Columbia University
in the City of New York
NEW YORK 27, N.Y.
OFFICE OF THE PRESIDENT

April 8, 1950

Dear Mr. Bruce:

Thank you for your letter and the compliment implicit in your request that I prepare a statement on the whole Indian Problem. Unfortunately, these days are so crowded with urgent official business that I do not have even minutes of leisure, and an adequate statement--I greatly fear--would require some hours of study and preparation. Under the circumstances, I am sure that you will accept my regrets.

Sincerely,

Dwight D Eisenhower

Mr. Louis R. Bruce, Jr.
National Congress of American Indians
1426 35th Street, Northwest
Washington, D. C.

Dwight D. Eisenhower, President of Columbia University, replies to a letter from Louis Bruce, April 1950.

A small portion of Louis's bio reads:

1945-1950 Member Board of Directors
Education and Youth Director
Dairymen's League Cooperative Association

Conducted marketing and employee meetings on marketing:

Conducted leadership institutes for adults and youth. Represented the Coop League on national and state committees at Congressional hearings.

Assisted in organizing Rural Youth USA; National Milk Producers Federation Coop Youth Organization for Indian participation.

Sent youth representatives to the United Nations Youth Council.

Was also active as an official representative with lobbying responsibility within the National Milk Producers Federation [a national association of milk marketing co-ops].

And the four or five years that followed the above were none too shabby, either. Between '55 and '59 he served as Vice President of Burke, Dowling, Adams in New York City. He was Account Executive for Delta Airlines, Allis-Chalmers, American Dairy Association, Gleem, American Can Company, American Motors (Director of Marketing Team), and Vice President of Compton Advertising, New York City.

Continuing Life on the Farm and a Rapidly Expanding Career

Anna Bruce had a busy life with her husband Louis, standing behind him in his numerous quests while they raised their three children. Anna held deep religious beliefs and thoroughly enjoyed playing the organ as well as leading the choir at their Church of Christ Uniting. While residing in Richfield Springs she still found it possible to teach Sunday school.

During the periods they lived on the Wikoff farm she oversaw the chores as her hubby necessarily bolted across the States. For years the farm consisted of 600 acres and hundreds of head of cattle, while situated on both sides of New York's Canadarago Lake. Tending the chickens, cows, pigs, riding and work horses, not to mention the crops of hops, corn, sugar beets and assorted vegetables left little time for keeping house. Thankfully she had the help of all those young folks her husband would bring to live with them.

Son Don relates, "Our house was like a dormitory. When we were growing up there were always Indians around and crazy things going on. And there would be white kids who wanted to get into Cornell's Agriculture course but needed a little background in working farms. Sometimes they'd even come back for a second summer. Dad worked for the Department of Employment and established a program with them. Those times were fun. We'd all play a lot of football out on our front lawn."

Charles, the first-born of the Bruce's three children, remembers a trip out west with sister Kate and their parents. "I believe it was when we went to South Dakota. Mom was at the wheel and she always drove so fast. Once another car passed us and she didn't like that so she passed him up again. She was a character," he added with a note of warm, deep love. "Mom was really a good driver, though. In all her years she only had one accident. She slid off the very icy Mohawk Valley hill and into a tree. She wasn't hurt and the car wasn't too damaged. But she was very embarrassed."

Clearly Charles felt a deep admiration for both parents, their endeavors and successes. Of his mother Charles says, "She wanted dad to be successful at the business end. She might nag and nag at him and he'd just smile and say, "Oh, Annie.""

Digging deep into his memory bank Charles said, "Oh how dad snored. It was on a trip once to Las Cruces when mom wanted me to sleep with dad in his room for some reason, but warned me dad was a loud snorer. How right she was. His snoring shook the windowpane. Seriously. It shook the windowpane. This quiet man!"

Another memory of his years back in Richfield Springs was going with his dad to the Dairymen's Youth Group. His dad was very special to him, admiring so many fine qualities. "He was not a loquacious person," Charles bragged. "It was enjoyable being around him. He was very strong. He'd take us camping." And certainly not to be forgotten was the period of being in charge of the farm. "When I got married we spent the summer there, working."

His sister Kate remembers the farm with equally clear vision. "When dad would come home for a couple short days from his job when he worked in New York or from his Washington office, he would be anxious to jump into work clothes and ride his favorite tractor. He would rise extremely early." Kate admits she, too, was an early bird and would join her dad on his various chores. Kate said, "I'd go to the barn with him. Mostly he wanted to be outdoors. It didn't matter what the weather was. Sometimes we'd be baling hay, or maybe he'd be cutting the lawn. There would be just dad and me, and we had so much camaraderie."

Louis with his father, Rev. Bruce, reclining against a hay rake.

"[Farmhand] Smokey was a kick," Don smirked. "He still talks about how mother used to put him in charge of me on Sundays when we went to church. I was a little kid. A hellion, or so he likes to say, and claims I'd run around the church while mother was playing the organ or leading the choir. He says I'd go up and talk to her." Don sat back in his rocker and closed his eyes momentarily. "Grandfather Wikoff helped build that church in Richfield Springs," he added soberly.

Other family recollections of church are the common occurrence of trying to leave the building and head for the car and that delicious Sunday dinner. Invariably someone would corral their dad; perhaps a Rotarian, a school board member, or a local farmer. Their dad would tell them to wait in the car; he'd only be a minute. Perhaps an hour later he'd reappear. Louis Bruce would never turn down anybody seeking advice or a chance to chat.

Those Sundays were clear in his sister Kate's mind, also. "Sunday mornings were different; they were very special. Yes, we would all go to church, but when we'd get home for dinner Dad would always quiz us on the sermon. Sometimes those dinners would turn out to be an airing of what the week would bring. Then suddenly it would be time to take him back to the train in Utica or sometimes to the Herkimer or Albany train stations for his trip back to New York or Washington."

Kate's memories rushed over her. She bragged about what a good athlete her dad was, consequently he enjoyed almost any physical activity. "There was a place called Public Landing north of Cooperstown on Otsego Lake where dad would take us swimming. We'd go there after haying and he'd joke that swimming there would save on the water bill. We'd do that rain or shine. How dad loved to laugh."

Something else she was happy to admit, "We had many mud games. We would get hot and sweaty from chores. We loved playing in the mud. A few of the neighborhood kids would venture over once in a while and play, too." She remembered the "darker" side, as well. "Once in a while we would be playing baseball or something out on our sprawling front lawn and a bad storm would come along. Dad would sit with us on our long, long front porch and wait it out. He sure loved being outdoors. At times mother would holler out to him, 'Get in here. You've been outside too long.'

"Weekends were a 're-acquainting.' I'm sure mom would have liked being taken out to dinner instead of staying indoors, cooking." Sorrowfully Kate added, "I think mom got a raw deal."

Her niece Bridget recollects that dinners at the farm with grandpa always brought him to the table cleaned up from his chores or playful games, wearing a golf shirt or a sports jacket. Her exact words were, "He spiffed up for dinner. Mealtime was always an important time."

With great merriment Bridget related the story of the farmhouse in Richfield Springs. "One year we visited there for Christmas and where the front door is currently, there was a tall window sill. It was trimmed with greens and a candle. We were waiting for everyone to come in and sit down for breakfast. Grandpa was wearing a wool sweater and he backed up right into the candle. His sweater caught on fire. He had a great laugh and whenever he'd laugh like that his belly shook. He was just wonderful. So warm. So compassionate." You could feel Bridget's sense of loss in the tone of her voice.

She continued, lovingly. "He would rub our backs and tell us stories. Always there were stories." She speaks of her many pieces of jewelry and all the artifacts he had given her and other family members through his countless years of travel. "I have a little ring which only fits my little pinky. It's tarnished now and has a little turquoise in the shape of a heart."

Recalling still others in the household, Kate said, "Grandma and Grandpa Wikoff lived with us on the farm. I remember dad ran into problems with Grandpa Wikoff. Dad would come home and want to upgrade equipment or conditions, but my Grandpa was a very stubborn, intelligent, gruff person. He didn't want anyone telling him how to run things." Kate explained, "The farm house had wood stoves. Mom and I had to clean out the stovepipes. We went to central heat, but that didn't get done until after Grandpa's death."

After his death Kate explained, "Grandma Wikoff was in a wheelchair. She was a real ladylike being. Very seldom did she talk."

Kate added, "Aunt Noresta spent every holiday with us. She was a very creative person. She could make anything out of anything. I never did know Grandma Bruce. Mom said she was a real lady."

But there were also disruptive moves as years swept by. Anna followed her husband, giving Louis the required moral support in his many causes. Through upcoming years they were to make their home in New York City, Chevy Chase, Maryland, Washington, D.C. and Arlington, Virginia. On those occasions when they could return for a few days of rest Don would have to have his dad's special little tractor in good working order for him. Don said, "It had to be 'good to go' when dad would arrive. Poor mom and dad. It was an eight-hour drive to get here, and eight hours back. That left very little time at home and there were always people dropping in to talk things over with dad. His private life was definitely not very private."

Louis was never happier than when he was on his tractor.

Throughout those important years Anna was his right hand, frequently writing his speeches. Don metaphorically claims, "Mother may have been in the back seat but she guided from the front."

One spring evening Don sat back in his rocking chair, narrowed his eyes and one could see the wheels spinning around in his brain. His mouth curled into a slanted grin as he uttered, "Mom was always on top of things. Heck, she was way ahead of us. I remember the time dad's schedule was so tight. There were a couple places he had to be at the same time, so he told me I had to give one of the speeches for him.

"Mom was waiting for me at the car to deliver me to the meeting where I was to represent dad. We finally took off, and after a very lengthy silence she asked, 'Don, do you know what you're going to say at this meeting?'

"Lord, I had no clue. I sat there speechless, not offering a word. Mom finally looked over at me, reached down on the seat with her right hand to pick up a small sheaf of papers. 'That's what I thought,' she said as she handed over my talk, no hint of malice in her soft voice, but with the slight hint of a wry smile crossing her lips. 'Here, I wrote out the speech for you.'

"Mom was always the life saver. She always had everything under control."

It was in 1957 that Louis founded the National Congress of American Indian Youth Conference in the Capitol. This he followed by founding the National Congress of American Indians and then had the privilege of holding the position of Chairman of the President's Advisory Committee on American Indian Affairs.

Louis Bruce's many jobs had him moving about more than ever. He was special Assistant to the Commissioner for Cooperative Housing, Federal Housing Administration in Washington, D.C. There he developed the first National Indian Housing Conference, sponsored by the FHA in 1959. He sought and developed participation in Co-op housing on the part of National, State, and local officials, and the banking and construction industries.

It was during this time of working on the Housing Administration in Washington that Eugene Rooks of South Dakota was given an assignment in Pine Ridge. Eugene's grandfather, Joseph Rooks, was also Louis Bruce's grandfather.

Eugene's memory is very clear regarding those days, and even earlier times. Also starkly sharp in his mind is the work of Barry Goldwater and his family in the '20s and early '30s. The lovely beadwork of the Navajo and Apaches had caught the eyes of the Goldwaters who then would buy large quantities of these crafts, to be sold in their stores in Phoenix and Prescott, Arizona.

Barry Goldwater, a friend of the American Indians,
with Louis Bruce, 1971.

Eugene lived in Phoenix for quite a while and then met Richard Nixon while they both, along with several Indians, lived in a boarding house. "We got to be friends," Eugene related. "He said he was going to make a career out of law and told us he'd help the Indians some day. So, as you know, when he became President of the United States he appointed Louis as Commissioner of Indian Affairs."

Eugene continued his oral dissertation: "Those were the days of anti-lots-of-things. Anti-communism, for one. When I told them I was born under Socialism, they didn't understand, at first. When I would recount what the government had done to the Indians, how drastically different life had become for us, they were quiet or would quickly change the subject."

Entrenched in the memory of Louis's son Don, are the sojourns his father had to make. Don stated, "When dad was working in Washington, once a month he would leave home on Monday mornings and come back home to the farm on Friday nights, an exhausting drive after a very full day of work. It left him tired over the weekend, and he had the same eight hour drive to look forward to on Monday morning, very, very early." But still he would see to it that things were running properly on the farm, especially after Anna had moved away with her husband.

And always the visits back to the farm were too short lived.

Don added, "In 1960, Mother moved to Greenwich Village to be near dad. There he was widely known as 'the Greenwich Village Indian.'"

Asking Don what that meant to him, he replied, "I always considered my Indian heritage more important than my Scottish background. Indians always had a deep reverence for their background. It was uppermost in dad's life." He added, "As you know, Indians and the Indian way of life and their welfare was always of the greatest importance in dad's life. And I honor and respect that heritage the most."

In 1961 Louis organized the first National Indian Conference on Housing, and was instrumental in changing regulations of the agency to provide more direct benefits to Indian Americans.

"Dad would speak incessantly about Indians and the conditions of life for them throughout the U.S." He stated, "Dad would say, 'Indians and liquor don't mix!' He'd say, 'An Indian is not a *positive* person around alcohol.' At some point some Indians procured alcohol and decided to kill all the white people. One of the truly great problems of the past was the many treaties which were made while under the influence of alcohol."

Thinking back, Don uttered, "When father would take a trip he could be gone a month. He'd visit a great many of the tribes, but especially the Sioux and Apaches. He met with the poor, the very poor, and the wealthier tribes. He visited White Feather which was Indian Territory at one time. There had been a great many pueblos around there. Our current missile site had been Indian territory."

Who was it that said *the more things change the more they remain constant?* In Havesu the mail is still being delivered by donkey. At the Alaskan islands the bush pilots still have hairy flights, dropping down onto a lake.

Between 1961 and 1963 Louis was Vice President of Development Services, Inc. in New York City. Here, under a contract to Lockheed and Monsanto, he promoted the LOCPAC, low cost houses. He achieved major sales success in the Middle East. Here in the United States he successfully supervised construction, financing, and management of housing Co-ops. And he won approval for the first high rise condominium which was built in Santa Monica, California.

In 1963-64 Louis was Community Relations Consultant and Education and Management Executive Dept. for the New York State Housing Authority, NYC.

He was Governor Rockefeller's appointee to implement new legislation relating to the developmental programs for individuals wanting to move into Coop housing in NYC.

He also conducted the required education program. He successfully extended the agency's effort to encompass education of public housing and Co-op residents through the State. The program stressed the benefits and consequence of joint ownership, while the Public Housing education program focused on effective means of redressing grievances and the development of organizational methods to insure safety and solve problems.

An Indian gathering. 1966

Tepee at an Indian gathering. 1966.

Horizons continuously expanded, and by 1964 to 1966 he added to his growing list the job of Public Relations Editor, Marketing Promotions Director of Mid-Eastern Cooperative, Lodi, New York. There he wrote, edited and published a bi-monthly consumer bulletin covering the affairs of the members of the Cooperative, its supermarkets and any national developments of importance to this chain of 43 Cooperative supermarkets. Added to all this, he conducted quality control and product selection studies. He also had overall responsibility for system-wide advertising; he developed opportunities for Co-op members to appear on radio and television to explain and further the Co-op concept. He developed and ran workshops to raise awareness and improve the quality of Co-op services externally as well as internally. He represented the Co-op at all national functions involving Cooperatives.

Through all of this neither Louis nor Anna forgot their kids and grandkids. High on their priority list were their visits home, laden with something for everyone. If it wasn't flouncy dresses for little girls and play stuff for the boys, there was bound to be some sort of surprise. And occasionally it was something repetitious to which they all looked forward. Granddaughter Bridget can still taste "those delicious cinnamon rolls." "He'd bring a dozen packages of them. We'd heat them up and maybe put some butter on. Mom always made lots of homemade stuff, but those cinnamon rolls Grandpa brought were so special." Bridget remembered he loved his jellybeans, too.

Never at a loss for work, new jobs always sought him out. In 1966 to 1969 Louis Bruce became Executive Director/Chairman of the Board of Trustees of Zeta Psi Education Foundation and Fraternity North America Inc., New York. His responsibility as Chief Executive Officer was to manage a multi-million dollar budget. Hence, a major effort was devoted to investigation of college student's relations during the Viet Nam era. Louis responded to student discontent with institutional involvement in the larger society, with Foundation and Fraternity pro-gramming and coordination of National-Inter-Fraternity actions. He courageously mediated inter-nal institutional conflicts on over 100 American campuses and 30 Canadian campuses.

Through all these years could Louis possibly have envisioned what tremendous honors and tasks awaited him?

Commissioner of Indian Affairs

Headlines of the *Indian Record*, (special edition, September 1969) read:

Louis R. Bruce Named New Indian Affairs Commissioner
President Nixon Sees New Progress for Indian People

The Department of the Interior made the following announcement:

Secretary of the Interior Walter J. Hickel, on behalf of President Nixon today announced the nomination of Louis R. Bruce, 63, of Richfield Springs, NY, as Commissioner of Indian Affairs.

Bruce, a member of the Oglala Sioux tribe of South Dakota, was praised by the Secretary as "a man of unparalleled qualifications, with the leadership skills and the desire necessary to carry out the Administration's pledge to assure the Indian American is no longer the forgotten American...

(*Indian Record* was published monthly by the Department of the Interior, Bureau of Indian Affairs.)

Walter J. Hickel, left, Secretary of the Interior, with Anna and
Louis Bruce at the Re-alignment of the Bureau of Indian Affairs
(BIA), December 1969.

President Richard Nixon issued the following
statement on September 10. 1969:

> During the Presidential Campaign of 1968, I pledged that my
> administration would help Indians to reach goals they them-
> selves had set. This emphasis on progress through partici-
> pation on the part of the Indians is now the basis of this
> Administration's efforts to make progress in every area of
> Indian affairs.
>
> Under the leadership of Commissioner Louis Bruce, the Bu-
> reau of Indian Affairs is now moving forward on programs of
> health, education, economic and social well being for Amer-
> ica's more than 500,000 Indians.
>
> Progress through participation means that the voice of the
> Indian will be heard on all questions affecting the life of the
> Indian. It is not this Administration's policy to tell the Indian
> what to do, but rather to help the Indian to do what needs to
> be done.

I am confident that the coming years will be a time of progress for the American Indian, a time for which he has waited all too long.

President Richard Nixon congratulates his new Commissioner, Louis Bruce

Louis Bruce, seeking a more responsive Bureau, then issued the following comments:

Since this is my first opportunity to officially greet Indian people, I want to share with you some of my thoughts about areas of primary responsibility, which I will be undertaking in the next several months.

I intend to continue and strengthen the free communication between the Indian people and the Commissioner's office.

However, as I stated before the Senate Interior and Insular Affairs Committee on my confirmation, I see the major task before me as restructuring of the Bureau of Indian Affairs to make the organization and the personnel more responsive to Indian needs.

As you know, I propose to do this through a number of working task forces composed of some of the best Indian and non-Indian minds in and outside of government. The key to the success of these task forces will be the Indian people involved and their willingness to work with me to reshape an organization to meet their needs and then to assist us in the implementation of these plans.

The major areas which we must concern ourselves with are these:

A restructuring of the Bureau at all levels by redefining functions and staffing to meet Indian needs. In order to do this, a thorough study of the Federal Trust Relationship must be undertaken to insure that the best services are made available to Indian people while maintaining a viable trust. The vast array of programs available to Indian citizens from other departments must be fully utilized through a closer working relationship between tribal, state, and local governments.

As we review these programs, ways to develop the Indian communities must be uppermost in our plans. This means that, where possible, program funding should focus on tribal needs and use tribal groups and organizations as the grantee agencies.

I believe that Indian people have good will throughout this nation. We must be able to capitalize on this by accurately portraying our problems and progress. Therefore, our task forces will concentrate on how best to do this.

In order to accomplish this major goal, I ask your fullest co-operation as I undertake to know the present structure of the Bureau to do the necessary homework to reshape our organization, and call on a number of you to assist me by serving on the working task forces.

Although I would welcome the opportunity to come and get acquainted and visit in your community, I must pledge all my major efforts to the task at hand. This means I will be unable to accept many of your invitations in the next few months. Where possible, I will be happy to send a representative and a message of good will.

I do look forward to meeting and talking with many of you at the 26th Annual Convention of the National Congress of American Indians in Albuquerque, New Mexico, October 6-19, 1969. At this time, I hope to make a detailed statement about my position on matters of importance to Indian people. When our major work is concluded with the task forces, then I will be available to attend many of the special functions throughout Indian country.

I have pledged my administration to a forward-looking policy of a Bureau of Indian Affairs which is flexible and responsive and in which Indian people are involved in decision making and implementation of policies and programs which affect them.

I ask your fullest cooperation.

Louis R. Bruce

The Bureau of Indian Affairs (BIA) stated in one of their documents that their "responsibility is the administration and management of 55.7 million acres of land held in trust by the United States for American Indians, Indian tribes and Alaska Natives."

With 561 federally recognized tribal governments, this was indeed a daunting task. The Bureau was formed on March 11, 1824. Originally a division of the Department of War, in 1849 it was transferred to the Department of the Interior, and renamed the Bureau of Indian Affairs in 1947, rather than Office of Indian Affairs.

President Richard Nixon with Anna and Louis at his appointment as Commissioner.

Louis's strides were valiant in his years as Commissioner. As Chief Executive of the Indian Bureau he administered a budget of more than five hundred million dollars and supervised a staff of 13,000, including regional and area offices. Information had to be distributed to tribal leaders, field offices, tribal attorneys, as well as many others. They were sent policy changes as they were announced.

Early in his tenure a statement was issued on BIA's involvement and development stating in very short part: "He immediately began to implement his policy goals and appointed a number of working taskforces to work with him and with Indian people to reshape the BIA into an organization ...In 1969 Commissioner Bruce went before the Convention of the National Congress of American Indians to state, 'I want to get Indians involved in the decisions affecting their lives...and their communities, without the threat of termination.' "

U.S. News & World Report on September 14, 1970, pages 68-70, wrote: "A New Deal Coming for American Indians." It concluded the three-page article, "Whether a 'new era' is ahead for Indians is still to be tested. In the past, ambitious programs have been launched, applauded, then sunk quickly into the sloughs of history. One difference this time is that if mistakes are made at least they will be made by Indians and not by paternalistic white men."

In May 1970 the National Council of American Indians voiced their support:

> In his effort to reach every segment of the Indian population Commissioner Bruce and his staff have traveled widely throughout Indian country from Alaska to Florida. He has spoken to such groups as the Alaskan Federation of Natives, the Northwest Affiliated Tribes, Governors, Interstate Indian Councils, National Education Conferences, employment assistance conferences, and has visited many reservation ar-

eas to find out what Indians are thinking about his many program proposals.

Commissioner Bruce instructed key members of his staff to contact Indian leaders throughout the Nation and discuss the proposed changes. Following that the official notifications were proposed for the BIA staff.

Thus the new policies and programs implemented by the Commissioner and his new executive team may appear to be a drastic departure in traditional Indian affairs administration; however, they are a natural culmination of consultation with Indian people by Commissioner Bruce and of promises made to Indian people. This is, in fact, the sincere result of honest commitment.

Bruce addressing one of his countless audiences.

On July 8, 1970 Louis Bruce called a meeting of the Superintendents, addressing them with his thanks for their support and cooperation. In his 13-page address he affirmed that, "we _have_ seen improvements and we <u>are</u> meeting the needs of the Indian people." He introduced the members of his new team who were in attendance, including Ernest Stevens, 38, an Oneida, as Director of Community Services; Alexander (Sandy) MacNabb, a Micmac, as Director of Operating Services; Flore Lekanof, 43, an Aleut from St. George Island, Alaska, as Director of Community Services; George D. Scott, 32, a Creek Seminole from Oklahoma as Deputy Director of Education Programs; Leon F. Cook, 31 Red Lake (Minn.) Chippewa, as Deputy Director of Economic Development; and others, including William (Billy) Mills a Sioux from Pine Ridge, and interestingly, the first American to capture the Olympic Gold Medal in the 10,000 meter run (1964). And there were 5 non-Indians in major posts in the new realignment. There were the Tribal Relations Officer, Intergovernmental Relations Officer, Legislative Relations, and he finally introduced his "able assistants."

Mr. Bruce sagely stated, "This last July 4th weekend, I know that we all probably heard statements of key officials and national leaders. Here in Washington, I was especially touched by statements of Billy Graham. In spite of his description of our troubled times, he ended his speech with a note of positive optimism and cautioned us to never, never, <u>never</u> give in. This is what I have said over and over — that though these <u>are</u> indeed troubled times, we must retain the capacity to visualize a better tomorrow, to have faith in the future, and let this faith be our guiding light."

Commissioner Bruce continued on in his own eloquent and forceful manner. He said, "I believe we can do much more to increase opportunities for all employees while accomplishing our goals for Indian people. With this objective in mind, I have asked the staff to rewrite the Equal Opportunity Program while reaffirming policy statements... Promotions will be made on the basis of merit...

"I know that many of the words you have heard have been spoken many times before in the Bureau. We have all been well aware of the Indians' needs for many years and have been working to meet them.... In our efforts, success may not be quick to come, and many long hours of work will have to pass before results are before us, but let us always work with an attitude of optimism and faith in our judgment.

"So now that we're all gathered here, and I know that among us we have a wealth of constructive ideas, let's get on with our task of pursuing a more attractive and acceptable life for the American In-dian."

The BIA staff, October 14, 1970.

Louis's helpmate and elegant wife, Anna, was also very much behind him, in spirit and in her gracious presence. Often she would invite these staff members to their 14th floor "crystal city" apartment. From this vantage point everyone enjoyed the awe-inspiring view of Washington, its dazzling monuments and striking architecture of government buildings.

The Bruces enjoyed their Washington apartment.

The living quarters served as both a private retreat from the workaday bustle, on occasions when the couple could arrange to be alone. Or it could be a place for them to share laughter, cocktails and Anna's delicious hors d'oeuvres with workers who rapidly became close friends. It could also be a place for Anna to sit in silence and write many of her husband's speeches. As time went by the complex grew with nearby buildings eventually blocking some of the spectacular view.

The Commissioner made time at work for his grandchildren, always teaching them. Here he is with grandson Richard (Rick) Huxtable 1972.

WILL ROGERS, JR.

Santos Ranch,
Tubac, Arizona,
Dec. 9th, 1970.

Mr. Louis Bruce,
Commissioner of Indian Affairs,
16th and Constitution,
Washington, D.C.

Dear Louis:

In sorting the family files, I ran across this picture -- taken when you appeared on my 'Good Morning' TV show in New York, way back around 1956.

Now that I am writing you, may I add that, in my scattered trips through Indian Country, I hear everywhere what a change in attitude there has been in the BIA since you took office. The only gripes I find are from the BIA old guard -- and that, in my oppinion, is the best compliment you can get. My Indian friends think you are doing a fine job.

So do I. Just stay in there and pitch. It is quite possible that, many years from now, the changes you are making in Indian administration will be reguarded as one of the most important changes in the last half-century.

Sincerely,

TV host of "Good Morning" show writes a complementary letter, Dec. 1970.

The Commissioner wearing headdress at Pow-Wow on Pine Ridge Reservation.

Commissioner (right) greeting his friend,
Area Chief Jerry Jaeger.

Secretary of the Interior Mr. Rogers C. B. Morton signing the
guest book of Commissioner Bruce.

Louis was also responsible for the Bureau's pro-
gramming and directly managed the tribal finances
as dictated by the special relationship existing
between Indians and the Federal Government.

A few excerpts from remarks made by the Commissioner at a meeting of Inter-tribal Indian leaders
in Denver, Colorado on May 21, 1970 are as follows:

> The BIA is being transformed from a management agency to
> a service organization. This means that henceforth the BIA
> will function where it can function best — as a source of
> technical and financial aid — not as the last word in Indian
> affairs.
>
> BIA Area Offices will be made fully responsive to Indian
> needs and expressed desires. Flexibility will be the new or-
> der at the area level. Development of Indian communities
> and tribal estates will be the objective...

The <u>trust status</u> of Indian lands is reaffirmed. ... [It] is the link that holds Indians and the Federal Government in a special and unique relationship. ... But it will <u>not</u> hold firmly to old and rigid ideas of how the trustee laws should be administered.

Tribes will have the option of taking over any or all BIA program functions, with the understanding that BIA will provide assistance or re-assume control if any tribe so wishes.

Thus far we have been talking about the relationship between the Government and tribal groups. But BIA will also take a role in problems of urban Indians.

The new BIA reaffirms its priority responsibility for meeting the economic and social needs of Indians living on trust lands and at the same time recognizes its obligation to be a strong advocate of urban Indian interests...

Indians make a stand for their urban interests.

Too bad the "frequent flyer miles" weren't in existence back in those days. With incessant travel by Bureau personnel, it sure would have made for great savings. On October 21, 1970 Bruce addressed President Earl Old Person and fellow members of the National Congress of American Indians (NCAI) in Anchorage, Alaska. (He had met with them a year earlier in Albuquerque, NM.) He referred to prior comments of accepting a task he knew would be difficult and at times unwieldy.

He had a way of thanking and praising people for their help and dedication, always trying to keep them uplifted. On this particular date he included in his talk the fact that he was serious about their housing, saying, "Let's set a target date when Indians will be housed as well as all other Americans.

"If we are serious about Indians staying alive, let's set a target date when Indians will have proper food and medical care."

With fire and determination in his voice he spoke: "If we are serious about any of our problems, let's set a date when they are to be resolved. It may be five years from now. It may be ten years. It may be more. ... Let us set a date when Indian citizens will have the same opportunities all Americans are entitled to. Let us fix a time. A time when the horrible cycle of poverty will be broken, so that a father may proudly watch his son or daughter again grow up in a society where there is true Indian opportunity.

"Let us fix a date — burn it into our minds and our hearts — then go forth, united, and tell the rest of our country — the other America — that we are ready, that we have a dream, that we have a plan, and ask the other America where is your commitment? Ask the Congress, where is your commitment? We are ready."

At 6 P.M. Sunday evening, December 13th, 1970 the Commissioner typed a draft and on December 16th he addressed the U. S. Senate, as follows:

STATEMENT BY LOUIS R. BRUCE
COMMISSIONER OF THE BUREAU OF INDIAN AFFAIRS
BEFORE THE COMMITTEE ON
INTERIOR AND INSULAR AFFAIRS
OF THE UNITED STATES SENATE

Thank you Mr. Chairman. We appreciate this opportunity to appear before you and explain the importance of my recent policy statements.

This new policy and the administrative realignment it entails has been constructed with the help of my new executive staff. Indians from every region of the nation who have actively been involved in Indian affairs. I believe I can best explain what we are doing by discussing the three main elements of my new policy.

Part one is the re-evaluation of Superintendents. In my 16 months as Commissioner of Indian Affairs, I have had literally thousands of interviews and discussions with delegations of tribal leaders about problems facing Indians. Many delegations of tribal leaders have made the journey to Washington at great time and expense. They have brought me problems that should have and could have been solved at the agency level. I have welcomed these consultations but have been frustrated. Too often my directives are ignored by field personnel who feel they know "what is best for the Indian..."

The second part of this effort is intended to put at the field level the greatest possible flexibility and decision-making authority. I feel strongly that tribes should be able to discuss their needs directly with someone with this authority...

The third major portion of this re-alignment is really intended to expedite the implementation of this plan...

To some these changes may seem sudden and abrupt — to others they seem generations overdue. To me and thousands of other Indian citizens they are long, long overdue. These changes were not sudden — they have been years and generations in the making...

This policy should not come as a great shock to any of you. Although it may have appeared to some at my confirmation hearing that I was trying to appease the Congress and the public. I clearly and unequivocally stated that the Bureau needed restructuring.

I have repeated or paraphrased this belief before many gatherings of tribal leaders throughout the country during my 16 months as Commissioner.

We are not changing the substance of any Bureau program. We believe that the only groups who can adequately adjust these programs to the present needs are the tribes themselves. I have long felt that we cannot require each tribe to fit into the same mold. What we in the Bureau are doing is posturing ourselves to respond to the tribes. These changes will make it possible for the tribes to design and execute programs that meet their needs.

Copies of this address were sent to all Tribal leaders and an Alaskan Native group, which answers some of the most frequently asked questions about their policy changes.

On December 28, 1970 the Commissioner sent a Memorandum to all Area Directors and Superintendents on the subject of Tribal Contracting. In that memo he stated, "...It disturbs me that some portions of the policy have been misunderstood and therefore, I would like now to clarify it completely. This is a valuable opportunity being offered to all tribes and thus, it is necessary that you are fully aware of its impact. If you still have any questions, I urge you to contact our office.

"The policy of the BIA is to make available to Indian people and Alaskan Native groups, the <u>option</u> to take over the administration of any or all programs ... Under no circumstance must tribes be pressured to "contract" to operate BIA programs....

"In order to assure that this major BIA policy direction is available to all tribes, Indian leadership is encouraged to deal directly with our newly established Tribal Programs Unit at the Washington Office. I have appointed my Special Assistant Billy Mills to head up this activity....

"I have stipulated that all BIA employees are forbidden from soliciting tribes to undertake contracts — each interested tribe must consider the possibility of contracting and make its own decision. Therefore, it is obvious that employee performance will <u>not</u> be evaluated on the number of contracts brought in. Instead, performance will be measured by the degree of support and assistance extended to those tribes who do choose to undertake one or more service contracts.

Louis R. Bruce"

NATIONAL CONGRESS of AMERICAN INDIANS

NCAI OFFICERS

PRESIDENT
Earl Old Person
Blackfeet

FIRST VICE-PRESIDENT
John Rainer
Taos Pueblo

TREASURER
Dorothy Davids
Stockbridge Munsee

RECORDING SECRETARY
Peggy Acoya
Sac & Fox

EXECUTIVE DIRECTOR
Bruce A. Wilkie
Makah

1346 CONNECTICUT AVENUE N.W. SUITE 312 WASHINGTON, D. C. 20036 202-223-4166
(Headquarters)

REGIONAL VICE-PRESIDENTS

ABERDEEN AREA
Alvina Greybear
Standing Rock Sioux

ALASKA AREA
Don Wright
Athapascan

ANADARKO AREA
James Cox
Commanche

BILLINGS AREA
Marjorie Johnson
Assiniboine

GALLUP AREA
Joe Herrera
Cochiti Pueblo

MINNEAPOLIS AREA
Loretta V. Ellis
Oneida

MUSKOGE AREA
Hiner Doublehead
Cherokee

PHOENIX AREA
Veronica Murdock
Mojave

PORTLAND AREA
Walter Moffett
Nez Perce

SACRAMENTO AREA
Erin Forrest
Pitt River

EXECUTIVE COMMITTEE

RESOLUTION

Whereas,   the American Indians have had to struggle for their rights

from the early days of subjugation by the Westward movement of a new

people to this land,

and

Whereas,   the United States has responded to the needs of the

American Indians through the creation of the Bureau of Indian Affairs,

and

Whereas,   the lines of communications between the American Indians

and the Bureau of Indian Affairs throughout history have never been

clearly open,

and

Whereas,   under the directorship of Commissioner Bruce, efforts

are being made to open those lines of communications,

and

Whereas,   presently efforts are being made in the Bureau of Indian

Affairs to recognize the necessity to involve Indian talent in the

Bureau of Indian Affairs,

1901 LAS LOMAS N.E.   ALBUQUERQUE, NEW MEXICO 87106   (505) 277-6041
(Field Office)

page -2-

Executive Committee Resolution, May 5, 1970

NOW THEREFORE, BE IT RESOLVED

by this Executive Committee of the

National Congress of American Indians,

that Mr. Bruce be recognized for his efforts in the direction

of more Indian involvement in Federal and State Indian affairs.

And be it FURTHER RESOLVED that this committee offer to

Mr. Bruce its assistance in obtaining and maintaining

maximum Indian expertise in those positions which direct

Indian programs.

Be it FURTHER RESOLVED that copies of this resolution

be sent to all interested organizations and agencies.

Passage of this resolution attested by:

Vice President

Date: May 5, 1970   NATIONAL CONGRESS OF AMERICAN INDIANS

Aside from shifting personnel across the country, Louis Bruce found it imperative to have a superlative group among his Washington office personnel. Alexander (Sandy) MacNabb was one such individual with a worthy background. Sandy was raised on Long Island, a one-quarter Micmac Indian. He enrolled at age 16 at Colgate University, followed by four years of service in Navy Intelligence during the Korean War.

THE WHITE HOUSE

WASHINGTON

January 28, 1972

Dear Louis:

Thanks to your splendid efforts, we have
set a new course in Indian affairs, one
that holds great promise of progress and
dignity for all Indians. . You are a valued
member of the Administration team.

Sincerely,

Richard Nixon

Honorable Louis Bruce
Director
Bureau of Indian Affairs
Department of the Interior
Washington, D. C.

President Nixon shows his appreciation for Louis Bruce
and his staff.

He then attended Law School at Washington and
Lee in Virginia. While there Sandy claims he did not
feel discriminated against, but rather he was made to
feel a little different.

Later on, at his father's deathbed, he made a promise to his dad that he would do what he could to help the Indian people. The balance of his life has been dedicated to just that, with the help of a loving wife and seven children. He has, however, included all minorities, not just American Indians, in his earnest endeavors. He developed jobs programs for all minorities.

W&L Law, a magazine published by Washington & Lee University wrote an article, "A Warrior Among Us," dated Spring 2005, in which it states Sandy worked closely with Civil Rights leaders in the South in the '60s, and, "another influential mentor was Sargent Shriver, best known for his role as the first director of the Peace Corps and the Office of Economic Opportunity. ...He is a member of the Health Law Section of the Florida Bar Assoc.... also active with the Health Law Section of the National Congress of American Indians..."

To be envied is his ability to converse in six languages, including Samoan. He has been on the Boy Scouts National Council and has been a member of the National Republican Club of Capitol Hill. It is, in fact, very difficult to keep abreast of all Sandy's activities. He is currently Commander for 2007-2008 of VFW Post 8469 in Virginia, as well as General Counsel for Narcanon, headquartered in Canadian, Oklahoma (for Drug Rehabilitation and Education Services).

Sandy MacNabb joined Louis Bruce early during his post as Commissioner of Indian Affairs, where both men pushed to circumvent the red tape which beleaguered the Bureau prior to Bruce's arrival. There was much work to be done. The "will" was great. Left to be seen was the "degree" to be accomplished during Bruce's term. So many worthy causes. Where did one start? How one continued sorting through the myriad tribulations of hundreds of Indian tribes seemed as abstruse as Einstein's theory of relativity.

First Lady Eleanor Roosevelt with Sandy MacNabb.

Sandy's efforts, along with all the other heads of departments set up by Bruce, were taken very seriously. On April 11, 1971 Sandy, as Director, Office of Operating Services, wrote a memo to the Commissioner and others regarding BIA Contract Procedures. He stated, "I am deeply concerned with the situation which the Bureau finds itself in regarding 'Buy Indian' contracting. BIA field, Central Office staff, and potential Indian beneficiaries have waited some four months for meaningful direction to come from the recently established Buy Indian Contracting Committee. The lack of guidance and procedures is directly and negatively affecting the implementation of existing Bureau programs as well as halting the flow of needed dollars into Indian income."

Section 23 of the Act of June 25, 1910, (36 Stat. 861; 25 U.S.C. 47), the so-called Buy Indian Act reads as follows:

> So far as may be practicable Indian labor shall be employed, and purchases of the products of Indian industry may be made in the open market in the discretion of the Secretary of the Interior.

The Solicitor of Labor wrote a letter on May 10, 1963 that, "the construction contracts between the Bureau and an Indian Tribe, the Tribe is not subject to the provisions of the Davis-Bacon Act and its related statutes, if the work is performed by the Tribe."

Countless pages of documents exist with regard to handling products under the Buy Indian Act. In the fall of 1970 the Bureau listed, for example: "This section (4) limits the advantage to an Indian-owned business, which otherwise qualifies, to simply meet the low bid if they have entered a qualifying competitive bid at the time of opening ... the following should be considered along with the other criteria set forth in the proposed regulation:

Will Indian people gain business and managerial experience?

1. If assisted for not more than three years, will the Indian business be viable at the end of that time?
2. What is the employment impact on the Indian community by entering into a negotiated contract as compared with the impact under a normal competitive contract?
3. If a high percentage of the Federal purchasing dollars remain in the Indian community, what is the impact on the existing Indian

business activities and is secondary employment created?

4. What intangible benefits are created, such as Indian pride, problem solving involvement, and a feeling of the existence of opportunity for those residing and growing up in the community?"

With further regard to the above Act there were listed such things as Verified Requests for Tribal Takeover. A sample listing is:

Albuquerque:

Zuni Pueblo –Wishes to contract for Employment Assistance and scholarship programs.

Ramah Navajos – wish to negotiate a gradual takeover of all BIA programs.

Aberdeen:

Pine Ridge – The Oglala Sioux tribe wishes to develop significant tribal control over the existing law and order contracts and to expand these. A formal request to contract the Lone Man Day School has been made.

Rosebud -- The tribe wishes to utilize certain BIA education and adult education positions as a funding source to coordinate all education programs on the reservation. Interest has been expressed in contracting for the operation of a BIA dormitory run in conjunction with public schools.

Juneau:

Area wide – Alaska Federation of Natives has an employment assistance contract. They wish to expand this and to develop social service contracts.

Note: We understand many village units wish to take over and themselves operate BIA day schools.

Nevada:

Nevada agency – Nevada Intertribal Council wishes to come to Washington to discuss contracting in general.

Phoenix:

Indian Development District of Arizona – wishes to expand contracts with BIA for foster care of delinquent boys at the Southwestern Indian Youth Center.

The point being made here is that the Buy Indian Act along with other "contracting" carries many mind-boggling complexities. Sandy MacNabb states, at the time of writing this book, that one of the greatest accomplishments of Commissioner Bruce during his tenure was his superb handling of details with regard to this Act. Sandy said, "Louie should be memorialized for that."

With further reference to Sandy's document, above, dated 4/11/71, it listed a number of suggestions to override the existing problems, among them, "required format for contract jurisdiction be developed; the responsibility of project or program managers regarding contracts be spelled out; that proposals be submitted to the Bureau; ... and that formal tribal approval be built into the procedure.

Signed: Alexander MacNabb
Director, Office of Operating Services"

The above is a mere inkling of work carried out at the Bureau.

Natural resources were obviously high on the priority list: gas and oil, its exploration and production. There were Environmental Regulations as well as Tribal Regulations. There were water and the many "rights."

And there were the trust relations. History tells us in the Middle Ages England had a legal invention known as a "trust." This meant that a parcel of land owned by someone was put in the hands of a person who was to manage it; hence, a trust. He did this for the benefit of another person — the beneficiary. Therefore, a trust was the legal device for the control of that parcel of land. These were handled through either oral or written agreements. In modern times, in America, these trusts can be handled through banks, trust companies, individuals or other means.

From this over-simplification of an old act, the United States has borrowed some of the old ideas and is bound to act in the best interests of the Indians and with good faith toward them. They are required to act toward them in a spirit of fairness and "trust."

If all this is not overwhelming enough, a sampling of the House of Representatives in their daily *Congressional Record* makes note of all correspondence reaching them. This example is their statement at the end of a workday recording the following:

EXECUTIVE COMMUNICATIONS, ETC.

Under clause 2 of rule XXIV, executive communications were taken from the Speaker's table and referred as follows:

539. A letter from the Secretary of the Interior, transmitting a draft of proposed legislation to provide for the assumption of the control and operation by Indian tribes and communities of certain programs and services provided for them by the Federal Government and for other purposes: to the committee on Interior and Insular Affairs.

The Supreme Court was not a stranger to the Bureau, either. Taken from the undated *Lakota Times* newspaper, (byline Tim Giago, Editor. Washington, D.C.) is a short portion of his article entitled "Supreme Court Declines to Hear Bear Butte Case." The article starts, "The United States Supreme Court refused to review an Eighth Circuit Court of Appeals decision Monday in which the appeals court ruled that the State of South Dakota was not interfering with traditional Sioux and Cheyenne religion by constructing tourist facilities at Bear Butte near Sturgis, S.D. in the Black Hills.

"Bear Butte is the principal religious shrine of both peoples and has been used for religious purposes since time immemorial. According to the late Larry Red Shirt, who filed an affidavit in the case before his death, 'the original instructions of the Lakotas (were) given by the Creator on a sacred mountain, similar to the way the Ten Commandments were given to Moses on the mountain'....

Relative portions of the actual text of the *FORT LARAMIE TREATY OF 1868* reads:

TREATY WITH THE SIOUX, BRULE, OGLALA, MINICONJOU, YANKTON, HUNKPAPA, BLACKFEET, CUTHEAD, TWO KETTLE, SANS ARCS, AND SANTEES, AND ARAPAHO, 1868

Article 1: From this day forward all war between the parties to this agreement shall forever cease. The government of the United States desires peace, and its honor is hereby pledged to keep it. The Indians desire peace, and they now pledge their honor to maintain it.

If bad men among the whites, or among other people subject to the authority of the United States shall commit any wrong upon the person or persons of the Indians, the United States will, upon proof made to the agent and forwarded to the Commissioner of Indian Affairs at Washington City, proceed at once to cause the offender to be arrested and punished according to the laws of the United States, and also reimburse the injured person for the loss sustained.

If bad men among the Indians shall commit a wrong or depredation upon the person or property of any one, white, black, or Indian, subject to the authority of the United States, and at peace therewith, the Indians herein named solemnly agree that they will, upon proof made to their agent and notice by him, deliver up the wrong-doer to the United States, to be tried and punished according to its laws; and in case they willfully refuse so to do, the person injured shall be reimbursed for his loss from the annuities or other monies due or to become due to them under this or other treaties made with the United States. And the President, on advising with the Commissioner of Indian Affairs, shall prescribe such rules and regulations for ascertaining damages under the provisions of this article as in his judgment may be proper. But no one sustaining loss while under the provisions of this treaty or the laws of the United States shall be reimbursed therefore.

Article 2: The United States agrees that the following district of country, to wit, viz, commencing on the east bank of the Missouri River, where the forty-sixth parallel of north latitude crosses the same, thence along low water mark down said east bank to a point opposite where the northern line of the state of Nebraska strikes the river, thence west across said river, and along the northern line of Nebraska to the one hundred and fourth of longitude west from Greenwich, then north on said meridian to a point where the point where the forty-sixth parallel of north latitude intersects the same, thence due east along said parallel to the place of beginning; and in addition thereto, all existing reservations on the east bank of said river shall be, and the same is, set apart for the absolute and undisturbed use and occupation of the Indians herein named, and for such other friendly tribes or individual Indians as from time to time , they may be willing, with the consent of the United States, to admit amongst them; and the United States now solemnly agrees that no person except those herein designated and authorized so to do, and except such officers, agents, and employees of the government as may be authorized to enter upon Indian reservations in discharge of duties enjoined by law, shall ever be permitted to pass over, settle upon, or reside in the territory described in this article.

An unknown discerning author eloquently penned the following missive. Indeed, his sage words are valuable as a prized painting. He titled it

THE RAPE OF BLACK MESA.

Dot Klish Canyon is a long way from Los Angeles. In fact, it's a long way from anyplace, unless you think of Navajo trading posts like Pinon and Shonto as places.

But Los Angeles and Las Vegas, Tucson and Phoenix, and even Washington, D.C. have come to Dot Klish Canyon in a big way. They have ripped across it to get to the Black Mesa's coal fields. They will strip mine the coal, then ship it to power plants being built at Page, Arizona, and Mohave, Nevada.

A few days ago I stood in Dot Klish Canyon and looked at the mess. The road to the coal plant smashed across the canyon twice. The bulldozers hit a steep ridge the first time, so they just turned around and rammed through another one. The double roadbed dams the wash in the bottom of the canyon, destroying the natural drainage. A Navajo garden downstream lies dry and abandoned in the sun. A nearby Hogan stands vacant. It is a scene of brutal devastation, compounded by the most careless scalping kind of non-engineering. It made me mad.

Why were Dot Klish Canyon and the rest of Black Mesa and the people who live there chosen for sacrifice? Hanging from this question is a tale of environmental tragedy.

It is a tale of the industrial octopus, created by the insatiable demands of its customers, reaching into remote places and tearing them apart. This is the hidden story of environmental destruction. It's what happens to people who speak quietly in strange tongues, to places away from highways and headlines.

Mario Gonzalez, one of the attorneys representing the traditional Indians said it is very difficult to win any Indian case involving land or religious issues. "The three main Indian religious cases brought under the Indian Religious Freedom Act have all gone against the Indians," he said. "If nothing else, we've shown that the United States Court system is not working for Indian and minority groups the way the Founding Fathers of this country envisioned."

The newspaper article continued to state that the attorneys for the Sioux and the Cheyenne contemplated taking the case to the United Nations." (Note: This happened in 1982.)

At this point it is interesting to quote a paragraph of *The Northwest Ordinance, 1787:*

The utmost good faith shall always be observed towards the Indians; their lands and property shall never be taken from them without their consent; and in their property rights, and liberty, they shall never be invaded or disturbed, unless in just and lawful war authorized by Congress; but laws founded in justice and humanity shall from time to time be made for preventing wrongs being done to them, and for preserving peace and friendship with them.

Of further interest along this vein is the question, "WHAT ARE TREATIES?" An explanation is found in the book *Indian Treaties* by the "Institute for the Development of Indian Law, Washington, D.C. 1980" The book opens with the comment,

Treaty is a word that Indian people have heard since their first contact with non-Indians.... Treaties are made because of the need for mutual understanding and agreement between two or more sovereign nations. Usually the subject matter of treaties relates to one of the following:

1. Peace and friendship

2. Military alliance

3. Boundaries

4. Trade

International law prescribes no set form for treaties. They may be oral or written.

Taos Pueblo Council

GOVERNOR'S OFFICE
Box 258 — Taos, New Mexico

July 28, 1971.

Dear Mr. McNabb,

The Taos Pueblo Indians are planning a victory celebration for the winning of their sacred Blue Lake from the United States Government by the passage of H.R. 471 and signed into law by President Nixon.

You are cordially invited to participate in this once in a lifetime event.

The Taos Pueblo Indians are deeply thankful for the part you had in winning our sacred Blue Lake lands back and we sincerely hope you will be able to join us on one of both dates of celebration. On August 14th and 15th, 1971.

So that we may be able to plan as efficiently as possible, won't you please let us know whether you can come or not. If you plan to come, would you like our housing committee to make motel reservations for you. (We are very sorry that we are not able to furnish housing for any of our guests.)

Sincerely yours,

John J. Reyna
Governor of Taos Pueblo

JJR/pre

A bureau representative is invited to celebrate a victory with the Taos Pueblos, July, 1971.

The Commissioner meets with Taos Pueblos, August 1970.
From left, Kim Agnew (Vice President Spiro Agnew's daughter,
Louis Bruce, Chief White Star.

JOHN EDGAR HOOVER
  DIRECTOR

Federal Bureau of Investigation
United States Department of Justice
Washington, D. C.

August 4, 1971

Honorable Louis R. Bruce
Commissioner
Bureau of Indian Affairs
United States Department
  of the Interior
Washington, D. C. 20242

Dear Mr. Bruce:

　　　　　Your letter of July 30th has been received,
and your kind remarks regarding our treatment of the
Indian Police Academy in the July issue of the FBI Law
Enforcement Bulletin are appreciated.

　　　　　My colleagues and I are pleased that the
presentation of the material met with your approval,
and we wish to express our gratitude for the splendid
cooperation we received in the publication of this article.

　　　　　Sincerely yours,

　　　　　J. Edgar Hoover

The FBI and the Bureau of Indian Affairs worked together closely
on various issues.

Countless meetings were held at the Bureau's headquarters in
Washington, D.C.

The extent of the enormous complexities of work at
the Bureau was no stranger to Louis and Anna
Bruce's daughter Kate Huxtable. She reflects wor-
thily on Tom Oxendine as, "the little angel who sat
on dad's shoulder, making certain he wore the right
suit for each occasion and that he got on the right
train or plane."

Tom, a Lumbee, was born in Pembroke, North
Carolina in 1922. In 1941 at the age of 18 he entered
the flight-training program at Lumberton airport, a
part of a federally funded program to train Indian
students to fly. Tom's younger brother Joseph
speaks of family pride when Tom would fly danger-
ously low over their farm. Very skilled, he'd frequently turn off the Piper Cub's engine and call out
to them on the ground. Thankfully the engine always
started up again. Tom became the first Native American to graduate from the U.S. Navy Flight School. He
served as a fighter pilot in WWII, flying 33 missions.

In 1950 he was recalled by the Navy to active service and assigned to various squadrons as Administrative Officer-in-Charge and combat flight instructor for jet aircraft. From 1962 to 1964 he was Deputy Fleet Information Officer, assisting in preparing information on all naval activities in the Pacific. By the next two years he handled the news releases covering the Navy's participation in air strikes in Viet Nam. Besides other duties he provided technical information for news stories on naval operations in the Gulf of Tonkin.

From 1965 to '68 he was Aviation Plans Officer, Director Plans Division, with offices in the Pentagon where he was responsible for coordinating public information with other government departments, business and industry, and the news media on special or controversial subjects. From there he was Public Affairs Officer for the Dept. of the Navy in Washington, D.C.

Tom Oxendine is welcomed as Public Information Director to the Bureau by Commissioner Bruce, 1970.

From 1970 to 1987 he was Public Information Officer at the Bureau of Indian Affairs, under the Department of the Interior, in Washington. Tom states his unending roles included establishing and maintaining effective working relationships with members of the national media, specialized groups interested in the organization's programs, and field office. He responded in written or oral form to information requested from the news media and public.

If this was not enough to keep him occupied, he directed special events, ceremonies, tours, and other activities intended to develop interest in agency programs.

Tom is blessed with an engaging laugh. With a chuckle he states he returned from the conflicts of World War II, Korea and the Viet Nam Wars without a scratch ... but got mugged when he came back to Virginia.

He explained that in those earlier days there were "persons of color" or "persons free of color." He said, "The way the Armed Forces dealt with segregation was that they segregated black people. There were no restrictions on Indians."

Tom's word of wisdom is, "Whatever you conceive, or think of, you can achieve — and never be afraid of the truth." He reminisced poignantly, "I left the Navy in 1970. In June of that year I joined the Bureau, working in Public Affairs, traveling with the Commissioner. From that standpoint I knew him very well."

In seeking an answer as to the Commissioner's greatest accomplishment while in office, it was quickly obvious there was no short, concise reply. Tom said, "First of all, the relationship [of the Bureau] is a government to government relationship. Not a national one in ethics. It's a statutory relationship. Roughly there are 300 tribes in the States, and a couple hundred in Alaska — the Aleuts, Eskimos and Indians, ranging from Florida to the Russian border."

Further explaining a convoluted set of problems, he said, "What these tribes have is a federally recognized tribe. They have a statutory relationship. If they have that, they have elected tribal governing bodies."

It is very evident that all things differ greatly from tribe to tribe. Some tribes are lenient in their ways and some are not. Within some tribes a member can be someone with very little Indian blood. For instance a Cherokee from North Carolina could be a member with 1/32 Indian blood; since 1962 it is 1/16. Other tribes are very restricted. "The management of all these things alone is extremely complex," Tom said, — the understatement of the day.

This fascinating and learned man further stated, "I had been in public relations in the Navy. I took the position that I was there (and in the Bureau) to explain things. Example: if we have an Indian family that is in need of help, you do what you can to explain to them that we have no relationship with tribes in their state, perhaps, so you can understand the complexity. The Snyder Act carries out the commitments that are carried out in the statutes. Commissioner Bruce clearly understood that. The problem is trying to solve it and make it better. Indians did not agree with it, entirely, and non-Indians did not agree with it, either."

Artfully Tom continued, "The way it was before Bruce came was, we had a single policy with Indians, all dealing with Indians as they currently exist. That policy the government had. It would clearly work in one part of the country and nowhere else. Therefore the government got a policy which the Secretary of State came up with. In Policy 638 tribes could determine their goals and the federal government would fund tribes. Commissioner Bruce brought in

Indians to work. Bruce made it work better, and it worked to a degree."

A favorite axiom of Tom's is, "It is a lack of information where the problems are." He was an invaluable asset to Louis Bruce's Bureau. Aside from having received extensive press coverage as First Native American to complete Naval Aviation Cadet Flight Program, he is listed in *Who's Who in Government* and *Who's Who in the East* and has received numerous Military Combat Awards, including the Distinguished Flying Cross. The *North Carolina Pioneers in Aviation* citation states in part, "Oxendine was assigned as a scout observation pilot aboard the USS Mobile. On July 26, 1944, he landed his seaplane in the midst of Japanese gunfire, in adverse weather, to rescue a downed fellow airman." Little wonder Commissioner Bruce wanted him on his side.

Meeting at the BIA office; from left: Commissioner Bruce, Deputy Commissioner John O. Crow, Deputy Assistant Secretary William Rogers, Public Information Officer Tom Oxendine, and Secretary of the Interior Rogers C. B. Morton, 1972.

In 1971 a 25 year old from Ponca City, Oklahoma spent the summer visiting Indian Boarding Schools around the country. William Pensoneau worked under the title Youth Affairs Planning Specialist. He was, however, past President of the National Indian Youth Council. He sought a way for students to air their grievances. In mentioning his reports, the Washington Post on August 1, 1971, page A4 states, "...life in the boarding schools often resembled episodes from *David Copperfield*."

Pensoneau strongly felt most kids don't get a chance. They feel intimidated by the whole Federal system. Even the picture of Nixon on the school walls was a message to them that the President was in agreement with any punishment they might be suffering. It made the students cynical and they questioned their place in the world.

Commissioner Bruce had placed Pensoneau in that position a year earlier, along with the above-mentioned Sandy MacNabb, Ernie Stevens, and his top team. While this early period in Bruce's Bureau had already produced many good things, there were, nonetheless, many frustrations with Nixon's Democratic Congress.

And there were those who thought of Bruce as a puppet, as can be noted in the following cartoon:

Who said Nixon pulled the strings?

As in all school systems throughout the country, there were bound to be disturbing situations. One such problem developed for the Indians at Chevak Elementary School on May 11, 1972 when it was completely destroyed by fire. The facility was a federally operated day school serving 160 students from kindergarten through the eighth grade, consisting of seven classrooms and a multi-purpose room including kitchen facilities. If funds could be made available quickly, the school could be ready to reopen in the 1974-75-school term.

The Bureau quickly made a survey of existing buildings in the area and determined that some local buildings could be converted temporarily and used as classrooms, kitchen facilities and dining room. In addition the Bureau bought three mobile "classrooms" and were shipped from Seattle to Hooper Bay. From that point they were transported to Chevak by military sky crane. This only delayed the opening of school a very short time.

On June 8th the Department formally submitted to the Office of Management and Budget a request for $3,550,000; this for an emergency that was "unforeseen and uncontrollable."

With further regard to schools, as noted earlier, Commissioner Bruce was well versed in education at all levels and its countless ramifications. It grew no easier as they considered the problems on a national scale. A 1972 document from the BIA reads in very small part:

> Today's enrollment in the BIA operated schools is made up of Indian students who live on reservations or pupils who have social, emotional or behavioral problems. Many of these latter students either are from broken homes or have not been able to cope with available public school opportunities. These children need more than a regular school program. They need schools with personnel who are sensitive to the cultural heritage of the student, an instructional program which will motivate the student and education support services which will enable the child to develop his full potential as an American citizen.

Educational Objectives...proposal for Fiscal Year 1973 [listed in small part]:

1. To work with Indian people in developing education programs which can be directly administered by: them either through tribal operation of the school by contracts; through an Indian school Board; or other means that they may desire.

2. To expand the BIA Early Childhood Education program to include the pre-school Indian child and to provide program continuum from Kindergarten through Third Grade. ...

   ...

8. To assist Indian tribal organizations to actively participate in the Higher Education program of Indian Youth through contracting for the scholarship function of the BIA.

The very lengthy report/study covers such items as the Proposed Program; Program Direction; (this includes involvement of Indian parents in programs at local levels, indicating an increase of $4.2 million request, to include staff, Indian School Boards, Contractual Services, travel, materials, equipment and supplies and transportation).

Also covered is Education Personnel Training.

To give the reader an idea as to the scope involved, we offer the following table and the Fiscal Years involved.

ENROLLMENT OF INDIAN CHILDREN BY TYPE OF SCHOOL SYSTEM

	FY71	FY72	FY73	FY77
KINDERGARTEN				
BIA	2,323	2,719	2,987	3,419
Indian School Boards	396	396	470	516
Public w/JOM	3,939	4,178	4,498	4,899
Public w/o JOM	4,272	4,367	4,479	5,061
Private and Mission	1,034	1,071	1,025	1,012
Not in School	5,347	4,993	4,909	4,795
Total	17,311	17,724	18,368	19,702
ELEMENTARY				
BIA	35,613	36,743	39,395	43,630
Indian School Boards	464	604	1,705	2,481
Public w/JOM	52,688	53,809	55,003	57,424
Public w/o JOM	32,395	33,445	35,032	37,967
Private and Mission	5,301	5,172	5,163	5,039
Not in School	1,488	1,406	1,171	895
Total	127,849	131,179	137,469	147,436
SECONDARY				
BIA	12,017	13,042	14,173	16,107
Indian School Boards	436	564	637	739
Public w/JOM	19,896	21,040	22,210	24,370
Public w/o JOM	13,812	14,843	15,493	17,585
Private and Mission	1,780	1,831	1,847	1,993
Not in School	3,571	3,468	3,100	2,761
Total	51,512	54,788	57,460	63,555
SUMMARY				
BIA	49,953	52,504	56,555	63,156
Indian School Boards	1,296	1,564	2,812	3,736
Public w/JOM	76,523	79,027	81,711	86,693
Public w/o JOM	50,479	52,655	55,004	60,613
Private and Mission	8,115	8,074	8,035	8,044
Not in School	10,406	9,867	9,180	8,451
TOTAL	196,672	203,691	213,297	230,693
POST-SECONDARY				
BIA Voc-Tech	1,106	2,085	2,900	3,311
Scholarship Grants	6,100	8,400	10,500	16,400
DORMITORIES				
Public Schools	3,666	3,784	3,855	3,731

Enrollment of Indian children

Details continued with regard to numbers and kinds of aides required; the teacher load to be decreased from 30 to 26 pupils; the increase in required monies to operate the 19 dormitories to be operated in 1973 for students attending public schools, (an increase of $1.6 million — the enrollment jumping from 3,784 in 1972 to 3,855). There were contracts with Indian School Boards, grants to

Public Schools, Post-Secondary Schools, and Higher Education. Here there can be a language handicap requiring tutoring classes. Many of these Indian students are attending classes with non-Indian students for the first time. Even students who come from public schools have had little experience in working with non-Indian students. This lack of experience can best be rectified by strengthening orientation programs, providing for special reduced size classes, tutoring, and remedial services, and in-depth counseling programs.

The BIA report also states:

> In order to maintain identity and pride in their own culture and to properly assist students in their new environment, colleges and interested Indian groups need to establish on-campus Indian Studies Centers.

> Colleges recognize the value derived from such programs, but faced with budgetary limitations, look to the Bureau for support.

> The Fiscal Year 1973 budget will assist 10,500 students. The level of Bureau support is dependent, in each case, upon the amount to be provided through other resources. In most cases, the Bureau will continue ... to be the prime funding resource ...

> Research indicates that 50% of the child's intellectual potential is developed before age 5. We know that the most significant teacher a child has is the mother, who cares for him during his dependent years; that the learning of the very young child must involve the total family, if it is to be meaningful and lasting.

> The Coleman report shows that the learning center, in which the minority child is a member, has greater influence on his achievement than that of the affluent child. There is further evidence to show that the gains the children make, as in Headstart, are not sustained, where the curriculum of the school is unrelated to the prior learning experience.

Another high-powered accomplishment was the Commissioner's handling of confrontations and constructive changes he made. He established the American Indian Policy Review Commission, an outgrowth of his work as Commissioner of Indian Affairs. He appointed Ernest Stevens Sr. as Director of the American Policy Review Committee, under the Senate.

Ernest Stevens, after retirement from this position, returned to life in the Dakotas, fondly recalling his days in office. They were housed in the old FBI building across the street from the House of Representatives. "The American Indian Policy Review report has been placed in the Smithsonian Institute," Ernie proudly admitted, adding, "During the days of the take-over in 1972 I was in charge of all the police in the Washington, D.C. area."

Work took off in many directions, figuratively and geographically. In 1970 the *Journal of American Indian Education* published an article (Volume 9, No. 2) titled "Bruce Lists Indian Youth Program as Top Priority." In it Clarence W. Bailey, a veteran reporter wrote, in part: "Youthful Indians are the most pressing problems of the Bureau of Indian Affairs, according to Louis Bruce who made the comments in Phoenix, Ariz. in mid-January during a four-day tour of reservations in the state, to the *Arizona Republic*. Bruce said his Agency is busy developing various youth programs to help teenage and young Indian adults become involved in America's problems. Fully 65% of our total Indian population today is under the age of 25. That's why we have to devote considerable time to creating effective programs for them ... to help Indian youths become involved in all kinds of activities, to develop leaders not only for the reservations, but in national affairs."

Sports obviously were always high on the Commissioner's priority list. He made the claim that in all his life he had never seen so much interest in Indian affairs by non-Indians. However, he also felt strongly that there would always be Indians who would never leave their reservations and intermix with the balance of the population. He could understand that some Indians would always wish to remain in the tribal structure.

One year Louis arranged for his son Don and daughter Kate's husband Bill Huxtable to have a stress-free five-day jaunt in Washington, including the Ironworker's Golf outing.

"We were like two little kids in a play park," Don chuckled. "We got in about 4:00 in the morning, bleary-eyed. Dad had a motorboat out in the Chesapeake waiting for us and we were to go blue fishing. That fishing boat was scheduled to take off at 6:00 in the morning. By the time we got to it we weren't feeling too well. We went down under the hull to curl up and went to sleep for a couple of hours." It was all so clear in Don's mind and obviously there was much more to this story.

"The captain wasn't too pleased with us," Don recalled. "He had his 'radar' working, finding the blue fish without much difficulty. The catch for our boat was terrific, pleasing the captain. After all, it's good publicity for others in the area to see a bountiful catch from an incoming 'boat for rent.'

"The blue fish were duly cleaned and packed in dry ice. We had a small plane coming back and wedged our boxes of ice-cold fish under the seats, nestling ourselves down for a nice, relaxed flight."

A frown crossed Don's tanned face. "It was a bumpy ride and we hit one of those pockets when the plane seemed to fall from the sky. Air bags dropped from their hideaways as passengers struggled to place them over their noses." Don took a minute to laugh heartily as he recalled, "Our boxes of frozen fish came out from under the seats and broke open. Did you ever see dead fish swim? We scrambled to gather them up, along with the ice, and hoped for the best."

Stern as office life could be, it occasionally had jocular moments. There was the day when one of Louis's assistants had his son visit, all excited to meet the Commissioner. Louis showed him his Seminole blowgun and target. They accidentally shot a dart. Luckily it had wedged itself into the couch.

Early living conditions for Native Americans could be crude.

Time and travel took many forms. One June he was able to fly off to the Dakotas to view the land he had acquired. Although there had been 900 head of cattle at one time, grazing here was not the greatest. At this writing there is a tenant living within the borders who must walk six miles each way for water.

At eight pounds per gallon, how much can be carried at one time? How much of it is used for cooking? For drinking? For bathing? For laundry? This grueling task is repeated many times for numerous residents of the general region.

For many there is still no electricity!

A highlight of Louis's trip one year had to be watching the annual Sun Dance, bodies moving rhythmically to the beat of the drums. Gerald One Feather was tribal chief at that particular time, feeling it an honor to have the Commissioner in their midst. Gerald One Feather explained that the Sun Dance is a personal prayer. He said, "The dance can be about all kinds of prayers: a prayer if you or someone you know is sick; a prayer if something is badly needed; a prayer for anything of great importance. The dance lasts for four days."

When questioned about piercing their body during the dance, yes, it is of great importance and accomplished with great pride. They can give back to the spirit something of themselves. They can sacrifice something for the good of the spirit which lives within them.

One cannot help but be reminded of the dance on the tenth day of Muhurram, a full half world away, during the holy Islamic holiday. A nearly 1200-year-old celebration commemorating the cruel death of two youths, young men carry through the streets tall poles, atop which are placed magnificently cut paper "mausoleums." They dance through the town streets for hours, stopping at intervals, picking up their tempo, wailing to the beat of their drums while simultaneously flailing themselves. The lengthy procession ends at the local cemetery. They bury these magnificently cut paper tazias (mausoleums) with all due respect and solemnity. (In days past these tazias were also cut from precious sandal-wood.)

There are, of course, other Indian dances, in fact six of them. Each has its own intent, each as color-fully performed. The public can view some, while others are private.

Discussing today's lifestyles versus very old cus-toms, Gerald said it was difficult to compare. The past is almost forgotten in some respects. Stories told to younger generations were not often recorded and sadly much is lost. The Sioux were nomadic people and after the onset of life on reservations, forced schooling for "some," giving up their native tongue, changing to the white man's clothes, how does one compare the newer ways as opposed to traditions of many millennia?

Gerald One Feather asked and answered, "What is left for today? Well, we still do some things like the old days." This wise old gentleman is currently on the Board of Directors of Oglala Lakota College in South Dakota, the second largest Indian college in the United States. "We like to dry meat," he said. "It's called 'papa.' They do this with any kind of meat they have available, cutting it into strips and hanging it up to dry in the warm sun, thus preserving it. Net-ting could be tossed over it to keep away the flies and insects."

The meat is very flavorful, it was explained, but perhaps a little bit more toothsome are some of the fruits still to be found: wild cherries, plums and buffalo berries, although the latter are not as sweet as some of the other berries. Another favorite of the region is wild turnips, prepared as one cooks other vegetables.

Just as life for the early Indians was not easy, nei-ther was it a bed of roses for Louie. Son Don recalls grimly, "Dad tried hard to work <u>with</u> the Indians, instead of dictating <u>to</u> them." Certainly these efforts were not in vain; many of his fellow Native Americans eagerly speak of his undying efforts to assist them and make things better.

There were also days of unusual events at the Washington Bureau. For a time during certain meetings a young woman would appear on the scene, steno pad in hand, nestling herself in a seat mid-room. She'd attempt to take charge while others in the room looked askance. Louis came into the meeting one day and asked just what was going on. He quickly put a stop to her domineering. Louis Bruce always remained in charge!

Bureau of Indian Affairs Takeover; Trail of Broken Treaties and AIM; And the Siege of Wounded Knee

As African Americans, Puerto Ricans and other minorities were rising up, searching for equality, Native Americans did likewise. In the mid '60s and '70s they numbered only 1% of the U.S. population. The American Indian Movement, (AIM) was formed in 1968 in Minneapolis by Dennis Banks, Clyde Bellecourt and a group wanting to address the issue of protecting urban Indians from police brutality and other incidents.

During the decade from 1968 to 1978 "Indian Sovereignty" came to the forefront of Indian politics and firmly placed on the government's agenda. Under Nixon, the government's response bifurcated. They advocated moving ahead with Indian self-determination, pursuing reforms as a response to the tribes' unique and individual structures. But on the other hand it sought with heavy-handed police and sometimes with the military to repress American Indian protests and activism.

For seven years, starting in 1968, all three branches of government took major initiatives in Indian affairs. Included in the governments response were the following: the Indian Civil Rights Act of 1968, the Indian Self-Determination Act of 1975, a major attempt to reform the Bureau of Indian Affairs, the Alaska Native Claims Act of 1971, the siege of American Indian activists at Wounded Knee in 1973, formation of the American Indian Policy Review Commission, and major rulings by the Supreme Court on Indian tribal sovereignty and treaty rights.

Until 1968 any protests by AIM were standard civil rights directed against racism in the region where the group had formed. Meanwhile, in San Francisco the Indian Center used as a meeting place for thousands of Indians had unfortunately burned to the ground. Some felt that nearby Alcatraz would be a good replacement facility. On November 19, 1969 eighty Indians occupied it, for 71 days, bringing the Indian rights issue to the attention of the Federal Government, as well as to the American public. Besides, it made the Indians themselves aware of their inherent rights to self-determination. Prior to that time the American Indian Movement received no attention in the Minneapolis/St. Paul region where the group had originated. However, when Indians arrived at Alcatraz, it is said, "they went global." Everyone was surprised by the media's attention. Heretofore no attention had been paid to the civil rights of the Native Americans.

The role of the White House staff in any crisis is of the greatest importance. The task force can be comprised of multiple Departments, depending upon the situation at hand: Department of Labor, of the Interior, or Health, Education and Welfare, or can include many others. The White House, however, chairs the meetings. In the case of the Alcatraz "invasion," a representative from the Vice President's office, Robert Robertson, made several visits. Much of the general public favored the Indians in their cause. California Senator George Murphy was in favor of making Alcatraz an Indian National Park. Political activists became involved, as well as visits from other well-known personages such as Jane Fonda and Anthony Quinn.

Involved in the drama was White House staff member Bradley H. Patterson, Jr. In his book *The Ring of Power: The White House Staff and its Expanding Role in Government* (Basic Books, Inc.) he thought of the Indian crises between 1969 and 1973 as a trilogy. The occupation of Alcatraz, Act 1, ended quite peacefully on June 11, 1971 when three marshals escorted the last fifteen Indians from the Island. Act II was the takeover of the BIA building, covered in more detail later in this chapter. Act III was the second Wounded Knee.

In the ensuing years AIM expanded geographically and with additional concerns. And then came the plans for the Trail of Broken Treaties Caravan. Dennis Banks, one of its leaders, advised, "We actually met 2½ weeks prior (to the trip to Washington) and planned the 20-point program we were going to give to Commissioner Bruce for White House consideration." Dennis said he had been so excited when first he had learned of Louis's appointment to the Bureau. Speaking in glowing terms of Bruce's integrity, skills and working for his people, he added, "When we first heard that Sandy MacNabb, Ernie Stevens, Lee Cook and a few others were going to work for Bruce, it was a great thing! We were very happy. Nixon was finally going to look at it all."

Of Dennis Banks, Sandy MacNabb unequivocally states, "Banks was one of the most lucid guys in the group. He had a good sense of humor. I saw him once at an affair wearing a blanket. The security people were there. I sternly said to him, 'Don't take another step.' Banks just looked at me. I said, 'You're wearing a size 40 blanket and you should be wearing a size 38.' We all laughed. Banks was a good guy. And very bright."

Regarding the actual caravan, estimates of participants range anywhere from 500 to 900 or more people, and from all parts of the nation. They arrived by bus, car and whatever means they had available. There were men, women, children, and in fact a few nursing infants. On November 2, 1972 they converged on the Bureau located on Pennsylvania Avenue in D.C.

The date of the caravan's arrival was carefully pre-planned. It was sure to capture the attention of the media, for they came immediately before the Presidential election. The caravan was also to "commemorate" the steps of the 1838 Trail of Tears. when thousands of southeastern Indians were forced from their homeland so that the whites could live there. [See the "Wounded Knee" chapter.]

Tom Oxendine is a fountain of knowledge, something of a parallel to a Presidential Press Secretary. To try to keep things in perspective, one must remember that "some tribes recognize people as Indians with only tiny fractions of Indian blood, while other tribes require high percentage or even total Indian blood. And some tribes are not even government-recognized." This makes proper funding all but impossible. Tom further advised, "They came to fix the problem. There are so many Indians: racial, ethnic, national. It upsets people who are outside the area."

Astutely, Tom explained, "What they (AIM) basically wanted was to get the Administration out of the Department of the Interior which holds all the public land; they control natural resources. It's what the

Indians <u>have</u> that they're interested in, not the people themselves. They thought it (the Bureau) should be in the State Department.

"On the other side," Tom continued, "the treaties that were entered into with the Federal Government were for control. The problem is in communication. Indian leadership is trying to get people to accept how things are. The Congress of the United States must carry out the Constitution. All the treaties were administered by the Government. The way to change that is to go through the Court system. Congress cannot go out and change things just because they want to."

With further reference to the caravan, Dennis Banks and his group, Tom continued, "They established that they would come in and they wanted to deal with the broken treaties that the government made with them. They don't accept all things, that the Congress can change the laws. The people took Wounded Knee and said we have a treaty that gives us all the land from the Rockies to the Missouri river." He added, "AIM said we have a treaty with the U.S. Government. Now most of the land is gone and we never gave them permission to take it. They took the Black Hills and our gold. Congress opened the land for homesteading. They encroached the land and people."

Dennis Banks advised, "We had no plans to visit the White House in the beginning. George Mitchell was part of the advance team, but probably it could have been arranged. However, President Nixon was out campaigning and not meeting anybody."

When the caravan arrived, some of the employees were gone. The travelers had been in touch with the office by phone. MacNabb recalls, "Lots of phone calls."

"The back door of the basement floor of the BIA building opened to the parking lot. Ernie was at his focal point there," Sandy vividly recalled, adding with great emphasis, "Ernie was passionate." Then in wistful recollection he said, "Only two presidents have ever done anything for the Indians – FDR and Nixon. Nixon gave us the license to do things."

Now on the eve of the 1972 Presidential election it was the intention of presenting Nixon a 20-point program redefining Indian relations.

Sandy MacNabb was out of town. Commissioner Bruce was out of the building. Sandy animatedly reported, "Arrangements were being made to stay in churches and other places. When we came in to work they (from the caravan) said they were sent to rat infested places. The first indication I had was that the group came into a school in Oklahoma, 40 or 50 of them, and they wanted to be fed in the auditorium. The department said the government will have absolutely no connection with the Trail of Broken Treaties. Our hands were tied! Problems started because they wanted to be fed by the Bureau of Indian Affairs."

Suzan Shown Harjo said organizers had criss-crossed the country for months publicizing the gathering, but the plans for the roughly 800 from 25 states were inadequate. Organizers said some of the churches withdrew their offers for housing. The lodging that was available was too small for the numbers arriving.

Suzan clearly recalls events in this way: "The Trail of Broken Treaties people converged on the BIA building on the 2nd of November, looking for help with the housing problem. The leaders met with Commissioner Bruce. It was the end of Washington's work day and few employees remained."

As in "Murphy's law," one must expect the unexpected and the outcome was, in Suzan's words, "GSA police clashed with the 'Trail' people in the lobby at the very time the AIM leader, Dennis Banks, was concluding a press conference out front. The GSA withdrew from the building and the Trail of Broken Treaty (TBT) people were barricaded inside."

In her memoirs 30 years later, Suzan wrote, "D.C. police surrounded the building and snipers took positions on the roof of the Interior Dept. across the street. ... This was only six blocks from the White House and connected to it by a system of underground tunnels."

Suzan explained that she and her husband, Frank Ray Harjo, drove to Washington that night. They were producers for WBAI-FM radio in New York City, and went to the BIA building as press. They stayed in the fourth floor "Iroquois Embassy" which was neutral territory.

She stated that an electrician proudly assured them that they were safe from outside intruders because he had wired the fire-escape with 40,000 volts. "When we asked what he suggested in the event we needed that route for escape, he quickly grasped the situation and dutifully undid his handiwork."

Tom Oxendine, on discussing the visit from AIM stated, "They came in one day. We gave them the auditorium which is in the center wing of the building. The building had once been the Department of Defense. The security for that building changed at 4:15 daily and they opened at quarter of eight.

"I was still in my office when they came," Tom explained. "They had a meeting and they asked the cooperation of the Federal Government. However, we can't have any involvement at all with the Trail of Broken Treaties. That's a federal relationship. We were not permitted to deal at all with them."

AIM, however, continued their meeting and eventually, "They found their way out of the auditorium, for bathroom facilities, or whatever reasons," Tom stated, "and flooded the building. My office was in the rear of the building and my window looked out to the Department of the Interior offices. At 4:00 I wondered how hard it would be to get them out of our building.

"At 4:15 in come Russell Means, Dennis Banks, Bellecourt and a few other leaders and said, 'We're not going to leave this building until we have met with [White House staff member Brad] Patterson.' " Patterson had met with them earlier in the day.

Brad explained that, "Our system of government is elective. It doesn't help people who want to be in leadership. They found that the Bureau cannot spend a nickel. The government would tell them something they wanted to hear but they misinterpreted what was told them. It was misleading but we told them something and it was factual."

Tom said they then asked if Assistant Secretary of the Interior Harrison Loesch had been informed. Tom said no and suggested Loesch be called. At that he turned and looked out his window toward the Interior Dept. building. Tom said, "As I was dialing Loesch and looking out the window, here come 55 helmeted police marching in ranks.

"Someone said, 'Here come the goons,' and started barricading the building. We managed to get our people out. I called Brad at the White House. He was a peacemaker and the police backed down. "

Recollecting all the minute details, Tom added, "The Department of the Interior tried to use the legal system to get them out."

Oxendine reports, "The Commissioner arrived and stayed overnight that first night. The Secretary for Public Land Management got him out the next day. It had been determined that no Federal or Government personnel were allowed to be there."

The doors had those big emergency exit bars on them and Sandy reported, "We brought chains in and secured them closed." (That must have been about the same time that the security guard had placed his 40,000 volts on the fire escape.) Then as an afterthought and with a hearty chuckle Sandy groaned, "One day a group of young Indians banged on the front door and said they were told to come on Thursday. It was Thursday. They came a week too late."

Then, not so joyously, he added, "All of us were afraid they'd trigger a riot."

What a predicament. The caravan "met with the press," Tom recalled, "and I'm sure they had so many supporters who were providing food for them, like McDonald's and many other places." (Brad Patterson of the White House staff explained that, "I kind of went back into Philosophy 101 when they'd find out that the Bureau cannot spend a nickel.")

Tom continued, "I met with the press. I was spokesperson for the government," He also added, "I was authorized by the Secretary of the Interior to go in and meet with them (the Indians). They said they were going to take over the Bureau. They wanted it taken away from the Dept. of the Interior. They said they don't give a damn about our people." Tom reiterated Ernie's sentiments along these same lines, which were a bit more colorful: "When you get s*** the first thing you do with it is turn it into fertilizer."

On a more solemn note Tom stated, "We said we're going to do what is right. We had done something with the Interior's approval and Commissioner Bruce had a close working relationship with the White House and Congress. Trying to make regulations didn't work. We couldn't get people in the department to go in with us to change it. Ernie said leave the contacts, and what happened was, they approved what we had done. We negotiated to deal with the 20 points and paid them $67,000 to return home. They had a lot of support from the Congress."

Tom concluded one of our conversations by stating, "I did not attend any of the meetings in finalizing the deal."

Before that payment could happen, things got out of hand with those hundreds of men, women and children who had taken over the BIA building. At some point, MacNabb advises, "The army tried to take them out of the building. Louie (Bruce) was there that first night. He said he didn't care what happened to his job, he didn't want anybody hurt. Hard to say how many were there, probably between 500 and 900. My goal was to prevent violence. I remember one of those nights when we were in a big meeting room and they wanted Ernie and us to draw up a manifesto. I said, 'We're on your side, but we're not conspirators.'"

Decisively, emphatically, Dennis Banks of AIM reported, "The occupation was not even in our minds. Not planned. We planned on being there two or three days and then leave. We were talking about how we could get backing."

Banks was most gracious and friendly throughout our discussion, adding, "We realized this was a major event, and the reactions would be far-reaching. We realized that. I had met with the leadership before I went. I said, 'You know, Clyde, this changes everything. How are we going? We don't know what level of strength they will bring after this. This will be an historic event.' Had that not happened I'm not sure if we'd still bring the changes, or if it would never have happened."

Sandy certainly admired the way Tom Oxendine always handled things, and especially under these most trying six days of occupation. He stated, "Oxendine was always cool. He'd say, 'Don't forget the pow wow tonight.'"

One can only imagine the level of concern — on all fronts. Here were several hundred people settling down for what could be, and was, a lengthy wait. Would the White House consider looking over the "20 points," all diverse in nature? Number 14 was Abolishment of the BIA; #15, Creation of a new office of Federal Indian Relations; #17, Native Nations to be immune to commerce regulations taxes, trade restrictions of states; #18, Indian religious freedom and cultural integrity protection; #19, Free national Indian organizations from governmental control.

They set up a tepee in front of the Department of the Interior and flew the flag upside down. The general public was on the side of the Indian, the Bureau reported, not on the side of the government.

Picture feeding infants, toddlers and young children and keeping them free of boredom. Picture all bedding down for the night, anxious for the next day and the good news it would hopefully bring. Luckily it was a large building with adequately good lavatory facilities. Under the very best of circumstances there were bound to be disturbances, frayed nerves, mounting tensions. Dealing with economics, social and educational issues is no small matter.

The situation became near violent after militants entered the scene. Unfortunately they became drastically destructive of the building, including the gorgeous works of art dramatically painted on the walls. The beautiful scenes of Indian life which had taken the artist so long to capture were totally and cruelly destroyed.

One of the militants was Russell Means, described by those who know him well as being charismatic and with a diverse background. Russell is a Lakota born at Pine Ridge who has worked in the movies, including a part in *The Last of the Mohicans*. He has been employed by Disneyland and has worked as a ballroom dancer as well as holding many other positions. (Currently he is founding the Treaty School and Ranch Enterprises, the emphasis to be on teaching students not in traditional classes/studies, but rather in the ways of Indian forebears.)

Sadly, typewriters were gathered up and piled as barricades. Countless five-gallon containers were filled with gasoline and placed along the four storied stairwells of this BIA building. Wicks were cloth and sometimes cardboard. Literally thousands of feet of film were strewn along with other flammable materials. Countless light bulbs were broken and Molotov cocktails contrived. MacNabb informs that the stairwells reeked with gasoline fumes. They got all the people out safely. One can only surmise how many would have died that day.

Suzan Harjo's memory is the same as others mentioned above. She and her husband were with Onondaga Chief Bill Lazore and Faithkeeper Oren Lyons in the "Iroquois Embassy" when they heard a voice amplified by a bullhorn say, "We're going to blow the building."

Suzan wrote, "AIM leader Russell Means, Oglala Lakota, was on the first floor, near the bottom step, giving a high-volume speech with exaggerated gestures that could be seen from a distance — part Hollywood-Indian sign language, part Arthur Murray dance-instructor moves.

"With a theatrical flourish, Means lit a long fuse to the Molotov cocktail and yelled, "It's a good day to die." A chorus of voices exclaimed, 'Bull***' and Harjo, Lyons and Lazore stamped out the glowing fuse until it was not only extinguished but shredded."

When the Commissioner's name was mentioned to Russell Means, now 35 years after the take-over of the building, his response was immediate, crisp and distinct: "I think very highly of Louis Bruce. He knew from the inside out of the rigid colonial changes, and he was changing the policy.

"As far as I'm concerned, Louis Bruce had been and always will be remembered as a hero in the American Indian struggle."

With disdain he changed his thoughts to other Indians who, "time after time are bending over to the will of the government." Russell brought up recent court cases, saying, "It is criminal. There is still genocide going on at the reservations. I am continually in a court because of it.

"There are two laws," he smirked. "We are a sovereign nation, and we are not a sovereign nation — whichever benefits the government at the time." Russell stated adamantly that the Asians, blacks and other groups are singled out and treated differently. "They cannot be prosecuted for things done on Indian ground, yet the Indians can be prosecuted for offenses."

He added, "Louis Bruce recognized all that back in the '60s. He recognized American apartheid. He planned to do something about it by hiring the 'lions,' that is MacNabb, Stevens, Cook and some others. We always knew that colonial apartheid exists. It's going to happen to us. It's going to happen to the Americans."

Then he looked back again to the days of turmoil at the Bureau, and once more with glowing admiration for Louis, said, "I remember sitting in an office. Did you know he gave us an office to talk in at the Bureau? AIM got the 'credit' for starting the BIA takeover, but there were blacks and other groups there, in on all the trouble. But we got all the blame."

Sadness returned to his conversation as he thought of their once vast and very productive lands. Surely he was thinking of the thousands of roaming buffalo, the lush grazing lands and other fruitful, productive property, since doled out to settlers and others. "There is no family farmer or family rancher since the '70s. They have been massively removed. The farmer and the cattle rancher are non-existent, economically speaking. And for those that do exist, there are no chickens or pigs. There aren't even many little cats or dogs. It is deserted during the day because the farmers or ranchers and their wives have to go out to work. I am 68 years old, and I've seen a lot."

This man, however, still harbors bright sparks of love and appreciation for that which has been ac-complished. "Louis Bruce was far-sighted beyond any of his contemporaries."

Suzan completed her memoirs with a glowing list of participants who have, since the Washington event, accomplished great things. To this list she added, "We might have missed the dignified struggle for Indian justice embodied by Frances Wise, Waco & Caddo, Administrator for the Wichita and Affiliated Tribes. We came from Indian communities," she said. "When the flamboyant stuff was over, most of us went back home to help make our communities strong."

Suzan Harjo, a Cheyenne and Hodulgee Muscogee, is president of the Morning Star Institute in Wash-ington, D.C. and a columnist for *Indian Country Today*. In that paper she completed her *Trail of Broken Treaties: A 30th Anniversary Memory* by stating: "Years later I interviewed John Ehrlichman after he had served time in prison for Watergate crimes. He had been President Richard M. Nixon's top domestic affairs aide and I asked about his Indian policy discussions with his old boss. He said there weren't any. He could recall Nixon actually saying only one thing during the occupation of the BIA building. 'Get those goddamn Indians out of town.'"

Looking at the above situation through different eyes, another highly placed Board member of AIM is Vernon Bellecourt with the phonetic Indian name, when translated, means Man of Dawn. He is of the Ojibway Nation, more commonly known as Chippewas. He is also currently the Executive Director for the Ministry of International Relations for the American Indians. He is president of the National Coalition on Racism in Sports and Media. "We are on the cutting edge," he said.

Regarding the American Indian Movement, he proclaimed, "We decided we were going to make a formal march on Washington to bring about change. The march was known as *The Trail of Broken Treaties.* What happened was Hank Adams and other activists got together. Janet McCloud was one of the leaders of Fishing Rights, for example. And there were others who came from Washington State, a group from Los Angeles and yet another group from San Francisco. The three groups merged at the Fairgrounds in St, Paul. They reviewed the 20-point manifesto. The document was visionary.

"We asked people to go into about a six-day workshop and come back with a language of how to deal with the issues. After about a week it was given to a drafting committee, and out of it came the document. It was to be presented to the joint session of Congress, and to the President, and to the American public.

"We embarked on a caravan to Washington, executing our right to present Congress and the White House a redress of our grievances.

"When we arrived in Washington at about 2 or 3 in the morning, it was decided we should look like one of the old Hollywood movies with their old wagon trains. We drove down Pennsylvania Avenue toward the White House and past the Capitol. Almost immediately swarms of state police and almost every sector obviously descended on us. They escorted us to a church that our advance team made arrangements for us to assemble in.

"When we got into the church it was horrible. All the men and women and the children were very upset. They said, 'We didn't come all the way to Washington to be sent into a rat-infested church.' "

With what must have been a churning stomach, Vernon continued, "We made a quick decision. The BIA building. The Bureau was to take care of Indian needs! Although this was not our original intention.

"We left early for the BIA. We had to park wherever we could find a place, in the back parking lot, or just anywhere, to the dismay of the BIA employees." Vernon indicated that was another of many predicaments, with still more to follow.

"In terms of the Indian Movement," he went on, "there was a sort of informal steering committee. We converged into the building. There was a loosely knit committee formed with Indians from across the country.

"What happened was, the occupation was actually a police blunder. The police over-reacted when people had gone back out to their cars to bring in things, like maybe diapers, or food, or some needed clothing. At first they were allowed in and out, but then quickly things got out of hand. The building was locked to keep people from going in and out.

"Then things got really rough," Vernon stated in disgust. "Adults and even children were beaten up. A man, Henry Wahwausack, was beaten on the head. He was bleeding badly, so naturally our people went into an emergency mode, and started to block the doors with furniture, filing cabinets and everything they could find to keep more police or others from getting in. They felt they had to take real action," Vernon explained.

"That whole affair was started by federal agents. The whole building started to deteriorate."

At this point Vernon's vision changed and he thought dramatically of the Commissioner. In the gentlest voice he said, "What I can recall of Louis Bruce is that he was a soft-spoken man. A very likeable human being." He stressed, "<u>Our hearts went out to him because he was the first Commissioner or Indian who was faced with this very tragic situation where an agency was coming down around him</u>. He tried to set up the meetings with the Nixon administration."

Returning to their actions, Vernon added, "We put together a delegation from the Six Nations and also others, and we had some very prominent people. We put together this negotiating committee who delivered it to the Nixon White House.

"One other thing I should say is that this was on the eve of Nixon's second election. This was also the time of the Watergate break-in which involved Ehrlichman, Mitchell and others on Nixon's staff and Congressional people, and Loesch. And here we were, dealing with people who were trying to cover up Watergate. So they were incapable of dealing with our problems."

Vernon recalled each detail as if it happened yesterday. He continued, "There was a new organization at the Smith Hotel and we invited them to come to the BIA. It was a difficult task of cleaning up and putting things in place. The Bureau had been ransacked. There was rubble and graffiti everywhere. They had taken wrenches and broken things. It was a horrible mess to clean up. The toilets had been broken, (and they were needed so badly with so many people camped there)."

On one of the interior walls an unknown person had written, "In building anew, one must first destroy the old. This is the beginning of a new era for the North American Native people."

With a very deep sigh, he added, "I was exhausted. I actually fell asleep at someone's desk. And then someone was waking me up. He said there were fires being started inside the building. I rushed out the room, took a couple buckets and poured them on the flames."

It would appear Vernon and everyone else inside had to constantly expect the unexpected. He related the story of seeing someone walking toward him in much of a daze. In great confusion he insisted he needed to get out of there. It was Bill Vetter. Vernon recalled, "I said okay and with a lot of trouble I was able to open up a basement window and I lifted him out.

"Eventually the negotiating team met with us," Vernon reported, but added a note of whimsy, now that time has passed and the events can be looked upon with a degree of humor. "Deep into the bowels of the White House they had hatched a plot to neutralize us. During a siege of the BIA building we captured two agents who had infiltrated the building, showing how the government works. We found one with a badge and belt he must have bought at a Walmart. He was wearing fringed pants, apparently trying to look like us. We could see right through the ridiculous 'disguise.' "

Once more, with a great sense of pride, Vernon spoke of Louis. "Even after that whole siege at the BIA I really admire the way Louis Bruce conducted himself. He never showed any emotion himself in terms of blowing up. He tried to reason with everyone. <u>I always wanted a chance to say something nice about Louis Bruce. Thank you.</u>"

And of course there were the more conservative Indians who disliked the handling of the situation and AIM itself.

Frank Carlucci has held a great many imposing position throughout his long, sparkling career, among them Director of the C.I.A. Sandy was one of a few recalling those highlighted moments such as Carlucci coming on the scene and saying they had $360,000 they would lay out. "We will set up a table and give them $200 or $300, whatever is needed [to return home]. When you get it all done, get the police to give you a hand."

Sandy explained, "We got seven different kinds of police. Frank Carlucci came in about 9:00 in the evening. They were able to get a police receipt for the building, indicating everyone was safely out."

Thanks to the auspices of the White House, special counsel Leonard Garment, Deputy OMB Director Frank Carlucci and Brad Patterson, a huge special task force had been set up. It consisted of eleven different agencies which could consider the points brought up for review. The decision was made that the Indian group would not be held liable for occupying the building, but they would be held responsible for damages inflicted and/or any theft. The new task force would study the situation and get back to them with any decisions. By paying their expenses for their return home, a possible greater tragedy was averted. The White House and staff had done a noble job.

Of the Commissioner, Dennis Banks had only high praise. He stated, "Bruce revealed to us confidential things but he was a very brave man to speak against the President and the Bureaucracy and how his hands were tied. I think the bureaucracy used this against Bruce. It smothered him down. It made him ineffective. It was a deterrent."

Of Means' actions during the takeover of the building, Banks stated, "I should have watched him before we let him in. He was always unpredictable."

Damage to the Pennsylvania Avenue building, which had earlier stood so proudly, was $2.2 million dollars.

On a different subject, Sandy informed, "Ernie and I were working on the Navajo reservation and needed some things to bring him into the forefront. Ernie was on loan to the Federal Trade Commission. There were 90 traders who were charging 50% interest. Hearings went on about that for several months. I was shocked and dismayed. Commissioner Bruce said, 'Lets make friends with the Chippewa's,' and we both went to Duluth. A guy, Audrey Skinendore, was called the Big Apple, meaning red on the outside and white on the inside. Skinendore didn't show up. Someone else took his place in discussions."

Bruce was a gem at sorting out problems and handling them with great aplomb. With deep pride Sandy described his boss, Louis Bruce, as "a man of great integrity."

However, after the solution of the BIA takeover and with Nixon's impending reelection, he desperately needed a fall guy for political reasons. Bruce's resignation was requested. Patterson informed us that political appointees regularly submit these papers as new presidential terms occur. Bruce's resignation was accepted, and Loesch was not reappointed, either.

It is said by those who were closest to Bruce and knew him and his work the most intimately that "more was accomplished during Louis's administration than any other administration. He should be an example to everyone. He was a moral and an institutional success."

Asking Brad Patterson how he now feels about the handling of the BIA affair 35 years after the fact, his reply: "I feel a good deal of warmth toward them, and a good deal of accomplishment. On July 8, 1970 President Nixon gave an historic message to Congress. The speech was written by Larry Price. Unfortunately the President's term ended in tragedy but in his domestic dealings he was wonderful."

Paterson further added happily, "Congress passed almost everything for the Indians. There were many different things. We took the initiative, and it was a bi-partisan success."

However Chris Gray wrote in a dissertation, *The Reconstruction of America's "Third Sovereign" Institutions, Regimes, and the Shift from Tribal Termination to Self-determination, 1959-1982*:

> ... Unlike either Johnson or Kennedy, Nixon was prepared to spend political capital to forward his agenda for the tribes ... and gave White House staff the authority and support to back Bruce's team of reformers ... but was unable to persuade Congress to go along with his plans. It is not clear whether this failure was the result of Nixon's conflict with Congress over budget impoundments.
>
> In any case, in 1972, the American Indian Movement occupied the B.I.A. headquarters. Angered by this action, the White House withdrew its previous active support. ... what was crucial was that the steps taken in these two years were in the opposite direction from all those taken previously. It was this that made these two years, in the recollection of activists who were involved in the change, an extraordinary two years in terms of changing the momentum of Indian policy.

And then there was the second big event at Wounded Knee. This is the affair Brad Patterson termed *"Act Three."* "When this incident developed," Sandy explained," Carlucci called Morton, Secretary of the Interior, and had a second briefing. The budget had tripled. After he laid it all out, the only thing he ever said about Nixon was that the President had stated tersely, 'Why are they making all that **** trouble?' "

This time at Wounded Knee there was greater fear of more violence. The militants were equipped with rifles and the 300 federal police had 15 armored cars. The White House was again in charge and sent Leonard Garment and Brad Patterson into a meeting with the Justice Dept. and other pertinent personnel. It was imperative the government handle the situation as well and as rapidly as possible. But as it has often been said, "the wheels of justice turn slowly." It took seventy-one days of arduous work.

An eye-opening footnote: The only place Indians are mentioned in the Constitution is in Article 3 (commerce clause of the Constitution). Territories are only mentioned once: Congress has the right to regulate territories.

Although Louis Bruce was no longer Commissioner of Indian Affairs, and had indeed been working on setting up his new business as President of Native American Consultants, Inc., he was nonetheless deeply concerned about the newest plight at the famous, or infamous, Wounded Knee. To round out this "trilogy" documentation, it was on the evening of February 27, 1973 when about 200 militant Indians were riding through the Pine Ridge reservation, stopping at Wounded Knee. Along the way they had taken 11 hostages. U.S. marshals, the F.B.I. and police were called in. Carlucci was again put in charge, by this time an old hand at demonstrations such as these.

Tom Oxendine was also sent out to Wounded Knee from Washington and reports that "Basically when the people took Wounded Knee they thought that was the government's responsibility. From that part of the Missouri to the Rockies belonged to the Sioux Nation, (as per the Fort Laramie Treaty previously covered). It would not be approved without ¾ of the adult male population. We never gave the government the right to do that, therefore if the government had lived up to it, we would be the wealthiest people, not the poorest in the country." (The government had taken the land with all the gold deposits.)

Tom's verbal footnote sadly reiterated, "It was a failure of the government by not living up to the treaty."

At the scene of Wounded Knee's siege, Tom reports, "We did a press briefing twice a day. There were about 125 news people there, 300 F.B.I. agents and 250 marshals involved on the site of Wounded Knee. We had sealed off Wounded Knee. We met daily with the people who had taken it over."

Tom further explained, "The government and the leadership met daily. They would brief me and I would put it to the press. We would give this information to the crowd every day at 5 o'clock and tell what happened. It was a one-sided thing."

Tom also pointed out that, "By making Indians citizens of the United States it subjected Indians to federal law, such as drafts, and many other things. The Dawes Act opened up deals with the treaties. It opened up land and homesteading. A lot of acts of Congress were negated. A lot that was in the Treaty. I would try to explain that to the Oglalas. You can't go in and take over Wounded Knee and expect all the other people to move out." Then Tom quickly added, "But they don't want to hear that."

Patterson had led the delegation of five from the White House, Justice and Interior Departments. A demand was made by the chief, Frank Fools Crow, for the return of the Black Hills to the Sioux. Patterson had to explain that only Congress could do that.

The siege of Wounded Knee ended May 9th after negotiations between the above-mentioned White House staff and AIM leaders Dennis Banks and others. There had been a standoff during which two Native Americans and one F.B.I. agent were killed.

Patterson astutely remarked, "We ended the three events in such a way there was a good deal of violence. The outcome could have been a good deal worse. There was both good and bad in it.

"We look back on it," Patterson said wistfully, "with a great degree of pleasure. The cases were won in court. A lot was always made of Native Americans; we speak warmly of those days. But we still have a long way to go!"

He added, "There hasn't been another President who has done so much for the Indians. We tried never to cut off anybody. We would talk with anybody. We never closed our doors. There were ultra-conservatives who didn't believe in talking to people like Banks, but we talked to everybody. It exemplified life. I don't think there has ever been a White House staff who has ever worked so closely with the Indians."

Tim Giago, a Lakota and newspaperman advised the Alcatraz event was not predominantly an AIM affair, but actually included more Indians from California and elsewhere who were involved.

Regarding the 1973 Wounded Knee Tim stated, "My dad used to work at the trading post there. He wondered why AIM didn't make an effort to help the 35 families who were burned out of their homes. Seven years after Wounded Knee Pine Ridge was declared to be the poorest county in the nation. It damaged the Indian people so badly they haven't recovered very much."

With the accurate boundaries of the Pine Ridge Reservation ever in dispute, the actual acreage remains a question, but is somewhere between 7,000 and 9,000 square miles, with approximately 25,000 living on the reservations and many more living nearby.

Following the 1973 standoff at Wounded Knee, Congress began to pass the President's agenda. And with the continuance of Indian unrest President Ford kept to the same agenda, redirecting Indian policy.

Mentor and Lobbyist

After Louis resigned as Commissioner of Indian Affairs, life was as busy as ever. He should have been content with his accomplishments, yet he was not one to sit back on his laurels. He had fulfilled a lifelong dream of helping his fellow Native Americans, yet it was an ongoing, endless task. He had managed to change the old policy with more Federal programs and having more Indians working. Now he was eager to continue his work through other avenues.

Louis established the Native American Consultants, Inc. (NACI) with offices two short blocks from the White House and his Management Resource Group office was located on Executive Boulevard, Rockville, Maryland. This was the official start of his lobbying for improvements in Indian life in the contiguous States and Alaska.

Native American Consultants was a private corporation whose stockholders and active principals were totally of Indian heritage. In a message he wrote:

Indian America has undergone a dramatic change in recent times. The Indian Self-determination Act has now become a reality, providing tribal governments with the support needed to improve the lives of their people through better health care, economic development, education and housing.

One of the most pressing needs is for health care and delivery. ... Yet we must not underestimate the expertise required in the specialization and complexities of health planning and health care operations...

Native American Consultants has accepted the challenge to provide the expertise and "know how" to assist tribal governments in implementing health planning and care services that are acceptable, assessable, efficient and effective...

I have committed our organization to increasing our capabilities in all aspects of health services. We have carefully screened and selected a nationally recognized group of experts. ... In addition we are establishing a National Advisory Board made up of leading Indians to guide us in our efforts to serve the American Indian Community.

Be assured that we will deliver services that are efficient, cost effective, and sharply focused on the real needs of Indian Americans.

Signed: Louis R. Bruce
President

Noteworthy is the clairvoyant admonition of Senator Henry M. Jackson, October 20, 1975:

The deplorable state of Indian health is a matter of record. No recitation of cold statistics can adequately portray the human misery and suffering experienced by the majority of Indian and Alaskan Native peoples on reservations and in numerous villages in Alaska. ...our national conscience demands that this deplorable health picture be corrected."

Native American Consultants documented the following areas of assistance they made available:

- Health Facilities Analysis and Operations
- Health Facilities Architectural and Engineering Services
- Health Programs Feasibility Studies
    - Cost effective studies

- o Operational Planning
- o Medical effectiveness studies
- Health Education and Training
- Services for the Aging
- Technical Assistance
- Contract and Grant Administration
- Alcoholism and Related Health Problems
- Economic and Physical Development
- Social Services

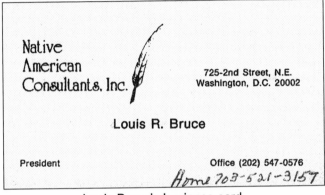

Native
American
Consultants, Inc.

725-2nd Street, N.E.
Washington, D.C. 20002

Louis R. Bruce

President

Office (202) 547-0576

Home 703-521-3157

Louis Bruce's business card.

The company provided technical and social support services. His principal responsibility was marketing. He developed a growing, balanced list of clients consisting of Indian organizations, federal agencies concerned with Indian affairs and other federal and corporate clients for whom they provided technical and management support.

Louis chose A. Patrick Hanes as his partner. Pat, of the Spokane tribe, was born in 1923 in Spokane, Washington, but lived in the Washington, D.C. area since 1967. He graduated from Gorzaga University and earned a Masters in Engineering from Oklahoma State University. In the Pacific Theater in World War II he flew 50 missions. After the service he became Acting Assistant Postmaster General. Along with other things, he helped design the zip code. He retired from the government service as Chief Research Engineer for the U.S. Postal Service. He established the Louis R. Bruce/Linda Hayes Scholarship Fund for Native American Indian studies at the University of Texas.

Sadly, Pat passed away in 2006. He left a wife and his three children, Dr. Patrick Hanes of Big Fork, Montana, and daughters Dr. Linda Hayes of Austin, Texas and Randy Waddell of Norman, Oklahoma and their families.

Both Louis Bruce and Pat Hanes were members of the prestigious Cosmos Club in Washington, D.C. This is a private club for intellectuals who have made sufficient contributions to society. It was this club that his children and grandchildren looked forward to visiting with Louis on their trips to the city. When in town on Saturdays it was almost a sure thing you'd be taken there for lunch, the only time non-members were allowed in the building. One would always wonder what fascinating personalities were to be met at that dining room. There were always such treats in store.

From left: Will Rogers, Jr., Louis's business partner Pat Hanes and Louis Bruce, June 1979, Washington, D.C.

Tom Oxendine, Trina Huxtable Iverson,
with grandfather Louis Bruce.

It was abundantly clear that Louis loved people –
and even more clear that everyone who knew him
held him close to their hearts. The "perfect size 38"
as his friend and confidante Sandy MacNabb termed
him, was always nattily dressed. It was invariably
one of the first things out of the lips of those interviewed.

On the other hand, his family prefers remembering
him as the man coming back to the farm for a bit of
R&R, ready to jump into casual overalls and open
necked shirts. A mental picture is usually their dad
sitting behind the wheel of his favorite tractor. Don
always had to have it clean and ready for his dad's
arrival home. In that spot he could temporarily be
free of the big city hassles, and the friendly little
village's drop-ins for chats or advice.

Louis's friends and co-workers carried their attrib-
utes still further. Sandy thought of him as a saint.
Asking his definition of a saint, he replied, "I've
known three people I think of as a saint. One was
Eleanor Roosevelt; another was the Poet Katherine

Anne Porter, and of course Louie. I think to be a saint one quality is to appear to be ordinary. Louie always appeared to be ordinary and never wanted any credit for anything he did. He was always kind and pleasant to everyone. Never a gruff word."

Sandy, a very learned Micmac, went on to speak of a French priest who said, "There is a moral evolution: i.e., you don't even <u>see</u> evil." <u>Louie acted and believed that everyone is good</u>. I knew only one other person like that – Ernie Stevens."

Grandpa Bruce holding grandchildren Rick & Trina, 1964.

Kate Bruce Huxtable's son Richard (Rick) advised that, "When grandfather left the BIA and started his contracting business, that's when grandpa was appointed to the Small Business Administration and received numerous awards and recommendations from the President."

Rick and his grandfather had been very close, just as Louie was with each of his family members. With the broadest grin Rick stated, "Grandfather and I were waiting for an elevator in one of Washington's really posh hotels. A well-dressed woman also patiently stood there, waiting. When the elevator arrived I started to get on, but Grandfather grabbed me by the collar, firmly holding me back, and without a word. The lady stepped in. I got the message. Grandpa was always very much the gentleman. And I never forgot that lesson." Rick was about 15 at the time.

Looking back in time, Rick stated that, "The days after the BIA were actually the most fruitful for Grandfather and Grandmother. They really enjoyed themselves and their friends and they flourished in the business world."

An old business associate, Joe Orth, advised, "I knew Louis after the BIA. I helped him form a small company that was originally set up for children's education. It became a small business. The first contract was with [the Department of] Education but we ventured into adult education, so to speak. It was to help Indian people to compete. He was the main-stay for many years. He worked with the Department of Commerce and the Department of Transportation."

Joe stopped to think over the many years gone by and the exemplary work. He added, "When you stop to think about it, he was the big position of self-determination. He believed that education was the best way to get people moving. Basically he was helping Indians find their way through the maze. The company expanded. We are still doing work today with the Defense Department and many others."

That was putting it mildly. Native American Consultants still has government clients: the Departments of Agriculture, Commerce, Education, Energy, Health and Human Services, Housing and Urban Development, Interior, Labor, State, as well as the Executive Office of the President. They likewise have contracts with National Aeronautics and Space Administration, plus the United States Postal Service.

Their corporate capabilities include analysis, assessment, evaluation and research, documentation, publication, graphics and transcription; engineering and technical support, program management and support, and workshops and conferences.

Partners Pat Hanes and Louis Bruce attending the Inaugural Ball, 1985.

Joe Orth stated emphatically, "That Louis and his partner, Pat Hanes, could do all that they did was very impressive. They still give a number of scholarships, mainly with the University of Texas.

Pat Hanes, seated, with Rick Huxtable.

"What impressed me the most about Louis," Joe confided, "was when we were doing a contract and we were walking around a Center in Wichita at a big open field. A guy was hollering loudly at Louie as he was dragging his young kid with him. He kept hollering and came up to Louie. He said when he was a kid he met Louie and he wanted his son to meet him, too. It was the highlight for me!"

He continued, "Once we had to write a paper on discrimination. That was easy for Louie. He told of when his father was trying out in Atlantic City for the baseball team. His mother was walking Louie around the Boardwalk when he was about 2 or 3 years old. Indians weren't allowed on the Boardwalk and his mother was arrested."

With a soft, pleasant sigh Joe stated, "We worked together a lot. Worked for just about every organization you can think of."

Joe's wife Penny still works for the same company that Pat Hanes bought from Anna after Louis's death. And now that Pat has also passed away, his children continue to run it. Penny actually started there in 1983. At the earlier height of the company they had employed 120, and while Penny's personal contacts with Louis were limited to company parties and occasionally running down to the other office to have him sign some papers, her recollections, like those of other personnel, were delightful. Penny had served as Director of Naval Programs.

Louis was also special consultant for the Department of Housing and Urban Development. As such he coordinated an effort to develop greater Indian accessibility to HUD and Inter-Agency conferences and committees, as well as Congressional hearings having an impact on Indian housing policies. He served on the American Indian Policy Review Congressional Committee in Washington.

Andrew Akins, a Penobscot, met Louis in 1971. He said, "I graduated in 1971 and went back to Maine and I wanted to see what I could do to help the Indian cause. So several other Indians and I went to Washington to see what we could do there. HUD and several other federal agencies were in existence at that time." With a note of disenchantment he quietly said, "<u>The only agency which would receive us openly was the BIA – because Louis Bruce was there.</u>"

As is the case with many other tribes, Andrew explained, "Our tribe was not federally recognized. But Louie brought in Sandy MacNabb and Ernie Stevens and he got us an appointment with the Indian Health Services. When they found out we were not federally recognized they threw us out. <u>They literally threw us out</u>!

"But I stayed in touch with Louie and he got us in with EOA. It was headed up by Ray Tanner. All the agencies had an Indian desk. Louie gave the tribes a chance to work with them and I was chosen to take an internship with them. Eventually we were able to get grants to get power, roads and so on for our tribes. With Louie's help we were federally recognized in 1978."

Andrew further explained, "During 1973 and 1974 the Maine Indians got a grant from a foundation. We decided to have a meeting of all the tribes not federally recognized. We formed a Coalition of Eastern Nations (CEN). They were all tribes east of the Mississippi. They opened an office in Washington. They hired a Lumbee to run it. We brought on Louie to act as a co-director; he stayed on for a couple of years."

With great emphasis he added, "Louie was very instrumental in helping Indians east of the Mississippi. He was a sweetheart of a guy. I just loved him. Without his help many of the eastern tribes would not be federally recognized."

To her husband's conversation Mrs. Akins confessed they loved parties at the Bruce's home. Not to be forgotten were Anna's delicious canapés that rivaled their hospitality. And then she admitted being impressed with the blankets American Airlines carried on their flights back in the '70s. They had been made by the Navajo and bore the name of Louis Bruce.

Pete Homer had worked as an officer of the National Congress of American Indians. He is currently President and CEO of the National Indian Business Association, a national trade organization representing 24,000 American Indian and Alaskan Native owned businesses. He stated, "The entrepreneurial spirit behind Native American owned businesses is the foundation upon which economic security for future generations of Native American families is built."

In an enlightening conversation Mr. Homer stated, "In the Equal Opportunity era we jumped on the coattails of the blacks at the time of their movements. Louis fit the bill — and the change. He had a lot of insight."

Pete rejoiced in the wonderful days of association with Louis. "I had left Arizona and was in Dallas a couple of years. Sandy came over and worked with us. We never ever lost contact with the Bureau. He brought us to the forefront. He was fantastic."

Looking back on AIM and the take-over Pete remarked, "Louie negotiated a good close to the affair. That went fairly well. In fact, we felt it went really well. As time went on they saw it made a change. If you took advantage of the movement at that time and made the correct changes, it made a big difference."

After that, Pete recalled, Louie went on to the American Indian Procurement and worked on federal contracts at the Consultants business. He made it a big success. They had one of the most successful programs Louie attended every meeting. We saw him all the time. He never really left. Whenever there is somebody like that, we need to honor him. I've talked about him in many of my speeches. What a scholar — and his wife was an inspiration, too."

Interestingly, Louis was one of five Commissioners who, with six members of Congress, sought to rebalance the deteriorating relationship between the government and the Indians. After hearings were concluded in all parts of the country, the Commission developed a series of legislative proposals reflecting a policy responsive to Indian and national needs. The recommendations of the Commission went before various Committees of the Congress.

Louis Bruce had mentored many, including John Meyers, President and CEO of Native American Indian Distributors, Inc. (NAID), a Service Disabled, Veteran Owned, Disadvantaged business. John recalls, "When I first came to Washington, Louis mentored me through some things. I served in Reagan's first and second terms and Bush's first as a political appointee. So there was a lot of national Indian politics I learned from Louis. He would help me with strategy. He was a marvelous mentor to many Indian people, especially those he felt would help their people."

John further testified, "NAID is very successful. Some things that I learned from Louis I applied to this job. It bore fruit. I am very well blessed. But it's a pity that more Indian leaders have not taken on the task of mentoring the young, even among the tribal leaders. They try to assume political power and don't think about their successors. Even when we have strong leaders, they don't look beyond."

In 1975 Lynn Engles, an Oneida from Wisconsin, came to Washington to serve as Director of Public Affairs at the Bureau of Indian Affairs and remained in that position until 1980. Crisp and clearly he said, "I was fortunate enough to meet Mr. Bruce after he left office. He was in office there at a time of great turmoil. Not only the Wounded Knee affair, but at the time of the Viet Nam and other struggles. He was a victim of circumstances beyond his control.

President Gerald Ford and Louis Bruce, 1976.

"Mr. Bruce became the elder statesman. He went beyond the stigma of Wounded Knee. He did so much for people like me after his turn in office. Mr. Bruce helped me so much. He was an invaluable source for me. He had a favorite oriental restaurant and he used to take me there. We talked about what I wanted to achieve. People recognized him for the wonderful gentleman he was. He was witty, funny and always willing to help."

Lynn moved from Washington to Portland, Oregon where he became Commissioner of Organization of Native Americans, which was under the Department of Health and Human Services, serving from 1980 to

1984. He said, "During Mr. Bruce's term of office he was very viable. He was well known on the Hill and with anyone who wanted to do business with the Indians. He'd get you introduced to people. It was so fortunate that he lived to such a ripe old age and was well known for all his help."

In May 1983 President Ronald Reagan appointed Bruce to serve on the National Advisory Council on Indian Education. He was Chairman of their Legislative Committee.

Louis and Anna Bruce in their Washington apartment with grandchildren Rick & Trina, Thanksgiving, 1987.

On May 12, 1986 the President announced his intention to re-appoint Louis to the same Council for a term expiring November 29, 1988. (Louis had, in fact, been an active advisor to former Presidents from Franklin D. Roosevelt to Gerald R. Ford.)

Louis and Anna's eldest son Charles noted his father had hoped he would join him in working on behalf of the Indians, however he advised, "I wanted to get into science. I was in grad school during the takeover." After his marriage Charles went into the Air Force in Albuquerque. Father and son would discuss the business and its varying problems. Charles remembers his dad saying to the Indians at the trying times of the takeover, "Don't trash this place; you'll only hurt things."

Charles remembers his dad was frustrated when he couldn't handle things. But he had very good rapport with young people.

Asked if his dad was hurt when he was fired by Nixon, he replied, "Dad wouldn't have played games. He looked <u>forward</u>, not <u>backward</u>. He was disappointed that AIM had screwed up."

Grandpa introduces young Trina to
ABC co-anchor Frank Reynolds, 1972.

Louis's granddaughter Trina (Iverson) is Kate's daughter who lovingly boasts that, "Grandpa used to bounce me on his knee from the time I was an infant. As a child many people got to know me. He would take me to receptions or to the White House where he'd have his picture taken with Presidents while signing some bill. I met Presidents Reagan, Nixon and Bush. He wanted me to get all the exposure I could," she proudly explained. "He'd take me to Williamsburg, and oh, he loved swimming and he'd get into the pool with me. He was a jokester and liked to play around."

A relaxed moment for Trina and Grandpa Bruce.

More importantly, she advised, "He was very big with my brother Rick and me, helping us to understand we could do anything." He had another side though and Trina admitted, "He was a terrible back seat driver. When he was Commissioner he had a chauffeur. When he was a lobbyist Grandma drove him around much of the time. When we'd go somewhere he'd pick on Grandma. She'd laugh and say, "You'd better shut up or I'll throw you out." Trina hesitated a moment, then added, "Maybe grandpa was too nice. People often took advantage of his trying to be helpful.

"He'd try to bring me into the Indian culture as much as he could. He'd have me dance at pow wows. In Washington during the summers in the Mall they'd have a big Indian affair with all their arts and crafts and pow wows and dancing.

"In my college years Grandpa had me working for his company during my summer breaks. That was in 1982, '83, '84 and '85. I worked in different capacities. For a while it was working on contracts for the FAA; and he got me a job in Health and Human Services."

Of her grandfather she said hauntingly, "He was a workaholic. Humble. He liked nice quality things, not splashy at all. And oh how he loved his raw oysters. On Fridays we would frequently eat out and he could eat his oysters. He loved to take pictures and never objected to anyone else taking his picture. I have some of him being draped with a beautiful Indian blanket." Trina is happy to now have one of these wool blankets in her possession. Adding to her collection are many artifacts: a tomahawk, numerous pieces of jewelry and other items.

Trina married and moved to Germany for seven years with her husband. They now are proud parents of two boys, 11 and 13. Does she have any regrets? Yes. Unfortunately her children never knew their great-grandparents.

Her brother Rick had fun recalling how he got started in the working world and that his grandpa would tell him to get into computers. "I worked with grandfather for about 5 months on one stint, and then there were others, but I was always in and out of Washington. We did a lot of events together." Perhaps it was the luscious aroma of his mother Kate's red raspberry pie exiting the oven which reminded Rick of lovely days past. He said wistfully,

"Grandfather would take me out to lunch with some of his friends. Problem was, they were always talking in acronyms. He had a tremendous network of contacts. I remember going to Watergate for lunch one time with a person from a very high-tech agency doing government defense contracts. Al Rawls was with us and the whole conversation was in acronyms. I was probably 15 or 16 and I didn't know how I could possibly get into the computer industry and show value to anybody.

"My first job was interesting. It was different in those days. I had just gotten out of college and you didn't have a lot of job prospects lined up. These days sometimes you have a job before you graduate.

"I received a call from this guy in Denver. He said, 'I understand you're looking for a job. Why don't you come down and have a talk with me?' I wasn't world-savvy about what was going on at that time so I went to see him in this really nice, big office. It was enormous, up on the top floor, in the corner, with big windows. I was thinking, this guy really knows something. Grandpa never ever told me who he was. He never ever told me that he had called this guy."

Intent on his story, Rick continued, "This was in '83. He sat me down, looked at my resume and said, 'You've got some good possibilities, a degree from Colorado State, and you come very highly recommended.'" That evoked a lot of laughter.

"He made a couple phone calls and in a few days I had a job with Martin Marietta at the junior level of computer programmers. It wasn't anything special, but when I started they gave me 2,000 pages of documentation and said the first book needed to be completed by the end of the week. And the second book needed to be completed by the end of the next week. No hurry!"

After five years Rick had an opportunity to go overseas to work. He spent seven years in Wiesbaden, Germany where he had his own company, an import/export business. He had originally gone over to visit his sister, and ended up being one of the first to bring personal computers to the military. Eventually he went to work for a contractor for the Army Air Force. He said we had 120,000 students in Europe and the Middle East.

There were always many events to attend.

Louis Bruce and New York State wrestling champ, 1977.

Louis Bruce with Olympic silver medallist Janet Lynn, 1973.

Ceremony President Anderson (left), Gary Roth, class President;
Louis Bruce, commencement speaker,
Hartwick College, 1974.

Don's daughter Bridget Roy readily recalls her
trips to D.C. as a very young girl. Her parents would

put her on a plane in Syracuse and allow her to fly alone to visit her grandparents for a week or so. It was quite a change for her, she admitted. "I was a little tomboy back at the farm, wearing scruffy clothes and wallowing in the pond with my two brothers. But mother always made sure I wore my prettiest little dresses in Washington, and act like a little lady. Grandpa and Grandma Bruce used to buy us pretty clothes. I was always in frills there.

"Grandpa's office was so huge and beautiful. I used to like to just look around." Bridget clearly loved reversing her role from tomboy to little lady. The happiness in her voice reflected her treasured hours and days with her grandparents, making her appreciative of her ¼ Indian blood.

Fondly recalling her "yesterdays" she giggled, "Grandpa just loved peaches. He had a little peach tree out in the back of the office building in sort of a little patio. One day he went out to pick a peach for himself and he got stung by a bee. Wow, did he ever swell up. It was awful. But he never stopped eating peaches.

"And his wonderful smell!" she quickly added. "I can never go past a sales counter and smell Old English After Shave without thinking of Grandpa. He always used it. It was always one of his Christmas presents and he smelled so wonderful. I just loved it."

There was never any doubt that Louis R. Bruce enjoyed life to the fullest. Through time he taught his offspring to make the most of each day and find their own paths through their lives. He reveled in their successes. He rejoiced in the hours he could spend at play.

His Mohawk friend Gill White, a leader among the Ironworkers, held an annual National Golf Tournament for Ironworkers and a few friends for about eight years. These are the workers who are well-renowned world wide for their skill at working 50 and 60 stories high hoisting cranes and bolting girders up in the clouds. For six generations, 120 years, they've come to New York to do this highly skilled and dangerous work. People call them fearless, yet they say they can be as fearful as anyone else; they learn to deal with it.

Gill advises he made Louis Bruce his special guest at the tournaments and Louis would invite his son Don. The event was so popular that the members went all out in the preparation of food. It was truly a feast to end all feasts. The buffet concentrated on regional favorite tribal foods with the golfers arriving from across the States. This delectable repast was the highlight of the three-day tournament. Feast your eyes on the following menu from July 17, 1980.

NATIONAL IRONWORKERS AND EMPLOYERS TRAINING PROGRAM

SEVENTH ANNUAL WILD GAME DINNER & GOLF TOURNAMENT

July 17, 1980

BROOKE MANOR COUNTRY CLUB ROCKVILLE, MARYLAND

Cover of golf tournament menu.

MENU

ROAST LEG OF VENISON
Alabama

MOOSE STEW
Wyoming

ELK BRAISED IN WINE
Colorado

ROAST BUFFALO CARVED TO ORDER
Wyoming and Colorado

TROUT BAKED AND GLAZED
Wyoming

WALLEYE PIKE PAN FRIED
Minnesota

ROAST CANADIAN GOOSE, ENGLISH STYLE
Eastern Shore of Maryland

BAKED DUCK STUFFED WITH WILD RICE ALA ORANGE
Eastern Shore of Maryland

BOAR ROAST
Tennessee

BEAR BRAISED
Colorado

CRAWFISH
Louisiana

SHRIMP
Louisiana

SMOKED STURGEON
St. Regis Indian Reservation

WILD TURKEY
Alabama

PHEASANT
South Dakota

FROG LEGS
Louisiana

Tee Off 11:30

*Assorted Side Dishes
and
Liquid Refreshments*

Their fabulous feast.

Eager to please their parents, the Bruce offspring labored with thoughts of the best gift they could give them. Their Golden Wedding anniversary was approaching. What would they most enjoy?

Their parents had always given of themselves. How about sending them someplace they could be "alone together?" They were intimately familiar with the United States. How about Europe? Sure. Why not London? They could move about at their leisure. It would be fun.

The departure date finally arrived. Everyone was excited for them. They were wished the very best. They were greeted by, you guessed it, FOG. The weather had to have dampened the spirits of the never-complaining couple. Always upbeat, they made the most of a dampened situation.

In hindsight Don admits the family judgment was apparently not the best, although their hearts were firmly entrenched in the right places. In the corner of Don's mind there will always be the feeling they could have planned something better. Perhaps that is an ever-pervasive feeling of all mere-mortals toward those we love.

The Bruces always looked forward to even short returns to their beloved home in Richfield Springs. Here they could bask in the never-forgotten countless pleasant memories — where echoes of joyful laughter swept down from their hills, mingling with the aroma of pickling spices or boiling grape jellies. The whipping shadows of wooden lacrosse sticks slashing over flat green lawns. "Grandpa" Wikoff, shotgun at his side, his sleigh laden with fresh milk, his lumbering horses plodding down lazy country roads. Memories of their livestock returning nightly to their barns. Dressing for Sunday church. Decades of leaving the farm for the Big City or Washington.

Louis and Anna at the Eiffel Tower, Paris

The Bruces had earned a long rest, but working for his fellow Indians was always the forefront of his being. Here in Richfield Springs they could have leisurely enjoyed their grandchildren and great grandkids. Even today the 22 rooms of their farmhouse hold many secrets of days gone by. To sit in their chairs and close ones eyes, one can almost relive their exciting past. Lives which had learned so readily to adjust to drastic changes: from meager reservation existence, to forced schooling, to higher education, to professional and political livelihoods. The Bruces comfortably mingled with the politically mighty and with the austerely depressed. Both Louis Bruces, father and son, accomplished unimaginable goals. The younger Louis's lifetime career of helping his fellow man is legendary. All America should be justly proud of these achievements — Native Americans and non-Indians.

As John Meyers succinctly put it, "I think perhaps the thing I miss most about Louis is that he has not been replaced by enough people he has helped. We don't see enough people doing a payback. We don't have enough of that type of person to take on young people and take on the ropes. Of all his accomplishments, perhaps that is the most important."

Louis Rooks Bruce passed away May 20, 1989. Anna Wikoff Bruce passed away on April 28, 2005 at the gentle age of 96. Funeral services and interment alongside her loving husband in Richfield Springs, N.Y. were private.

Both are sadly missed and joyfully remembered.

AWARDS

Freedom Foundation Award 1949. Presented at Valley Forge by General Dwight D. Eisenhower for article "What America Means to Me," published in *American Magazine* and *Readers Digest.*

Indian Council Fire Achievement Award 1952

National Boy Scout Silver Buffalo Award 1972

Syracuse University Alumni, Outstanding Citizen Award 1970

Otsego County Bar Association, Liberty Bell Award

Purdue University Students, Outstanding Citizens Award

Syracuse University, Outstanding Letterman of Distinction Award

Honorary Doctor's Degree, Clarkson College

Honorary Doctor's Degree, Navajo College, Albuquerque, N.M.

Other recognition Listed in the following publications:

Who's Who in America
Who's Who in the East
Who's Who in the Government
Who's Who in the World

Former top advisor on American Indian Affairs to Presidents:

Franklin D. Roosevelt
Harry S. Truman
Dwight D. Eisenhower
John F. Kennedy
Richard M. Nixon
Gerald R. Ford

Thistle Publishing

Publisher of selected books of distinction...

...on a variety of topics...

...by exceptional authors.

Order Form

 Thistle Publishing
11985 Cherokee Circle, Suite 1800
Shelby Twp., MI 48315
www.thistlepub.com

☐ I'm enclosing $ _____. Please send me the following books and publications:

__ *Chief of the Chiefs: Louis Rooks Bruce, Mohawk/Sioux, Commissioner of Indian Affairs, and Lobbyist.* (paperback) $16.95

__ *Eddie Elias: PBA founder merchandized sports, corporate, TV Worlds.* (paperback) $14.95

__ *Steadfast the Lamp.* (hardcover) $24.95

__ *Virgin Princess: An historic novel of Mewar (Udaipur, India)–the world's oldest dynasty.* (paperback) $15.95

__ *Remember When.* (hardcover)

Shipping: Please add $5 for USPS Priority shipping.

Sales tax: Please add 6% for orders shipped to a Michigan address.

Name: _____

Address: _____

_____

City: _____ State: _____ Zip: _____

Email address: _____

Visit us on the web at www.thistlepub.com.